Brother Lawrence of the Resurrection, OCD
(Nicolas Herman)

Writings and Conversations
On the Practice
Of the Presence of God

Brother Lawrence of the Resurrection, OCD
(Nicolas Herman)

Writings and Conversations
On the Practice
Of the Presence of God

Critical Edition by Conrad De Meester, OCD

Translated by Salvatore Sciurba, OCD

With a Foreword to the American Edition by
Gerald G. May, M.D.

ICS Publications
Institute of Carmelite Studies
Washington, D.C.
1994

The original French edition of this work
was published by Les Éditions du Cerf under the title
Écrits et entretiens sur la pratique de la Présence de Dieu
© Les Éditions du Cerf, 1991 (for all French-speaking countries)

Translation authorized by Conrad De Meester
English translation copyright
©Washington Province of Discalced Carmelites, Inc. 1994

ICS Publications
2131 Lincoln Road NE
Washington, DC 20002-1199

Typeset and produced in the U.S.A.

Library of Congress Cataloging-in-Publication Data

Lawrence, of the Resurrection, Brother, 1611-1691.
[Works. English. 1993]
Writings and conversations on the practice of the presence of God/
Brother Lawrence of the Resurrection (Nicolas Herman);
critical edition by Conrad De Meester; translated by Salvatore Sciurba;
with a foreword to the American edition by Gerald G. May.
p.   cm.
Includes bibliographical references.
ISBN: 0-935216-21-9
1. Spiritual life—Catholic Church—Early works to 1800.
2. Catholic Church—Doctrines. I. De Meester, Conrad. II. Title.
BX2349.L37   1993
248.4'82—dc20   93-2444
                                                                    CIP

TABLE OF CONTENTS

Abbreviations   vii

Foreword to the American Edition   ix

Foreword to the French Edition   xiii

Translator's Preface   xv

GENERAL INTRODUCTION   xvii
    Biographical Sketch   xviii
    Writings and Conversations   xxiii
    Various French Editions   xxiv
    Joseph de Beaufort, the Anonymous Biographer-Editor   xxx
    Brother Lawrence's International Influence   xxxii
    Significance of Brother Lawrence's Writings   xxxiv

I. EULOGY
    Introductory Note to the Eulogy   3
    Text of Eulogy   5

II. SPIRITUAL MAXIMS
    Introductory Note to the Spiritual Maxims   31
    1. [Principles]   35
    2. Practices Necessary to Attain the Spiritual Life   36
    3. How We Must Adore God in Spirit and in Truth   38
    4. Union of the Soul With God   38
    5. On the Presence of God   39
    6. Means to Acquire the Presence of God   41
    7. Benefits of the Presence of God   42

III. LETTERS
Introductory Note to the Letters   47
Text of the Letters   49

IV. CONVERSATIONS
Introductory Note to the Conversations   87
First Conversation   89
Second Conversation   91
Third Conversation   95
Fourth Conversation   97

V. THE PRACTICE OF THE PRESENCE OF GOD
Introductory Note to the Practice   103
Text of the Practice of the Presence of God   105

VI. THE WAYS OF BROTHER LAWRENCE
Introductory Note to the Ways   111
Text of the Ways of Brother Lawrence   113

APPENDICES
I. Brother Lawrence's Monastery in Paris   129
II. A Letter by Joseph de Beaufort on the "Life" of Brother Lawrence   137
III. Brother Lawrence in the Bossuet-Fénelon Controversy   151

SELECT BIBLIOGRAPHY   193

ABBREVIATIONS

The following abbreviations are used for cross-references to the documents contained in this volume:

EL = Eulogy   SM = Spiritual Maxims
CN = Conversations   W = Ways of Brother Lawrence
L = Letters

The numbers following these abbreviations refer to the enumeration in this edition. For example, CN 3 refers to the third paragraph of the *Conversations,* on p. 89; EL 12 refers to the twelfth paragraph of the *Eulogy,* on p. 7.

All quotations from **St. John of the Cross** are taken from *The Collected Works of St. John of the Cross,* trans. Kieran Kavanaugh and Otilio Rodriguez, rev. ed. (Washington, DC: ICS Publications, 1991). For his major works, the following abbreviations are used:

Ascent = Ascent of Mount Carmel
Canticle = Spiritual Canticle
Flame = Living Flame of Love
Night = Dark Night

In references to the *Ascent* and *Night,* the first number indicates the book. Also, references to John's Letters are based on the numbering in this revised Kavanaugh/Rodriguez translation, which sometimes differs from the numbering in other editions.

Similarly, all quotations from **St. Teresa of Jesus** are taken from *The Collected Works of St. Teresa of Avila,* trans. Kieran Kavanaugh and Otilio Rodriguez, 3 vols. (Washington, DC: ICS Publications, 1976–1985). For her major works, the following abbreviations are used:

Castle = Interior Castle
Foundations = Book of Foundations
Life = Book of Her Life
Way = Way of Perfection

In references to the *Castle,* the first number refers to the "dwelling place."

Foreword to the American Edition

At its core, the spiritual life is very simple. Jesus told his disciples they needed to become like little children to enter the reign of heaven (Mt 18:3). Moses told the people of Israel that the Word was not far from them, that it was already in their mouths and hearts (Dt 30:14). Life with God, then, does not require great theological sophistication; it is for everyone. Nor is our spiritual life restricted to hallowed places and mountaintop moments. It is the simple essence of living, moving, and having our being in God in every present moment, wherever we find ourselves, whatever we are doing (Acts 17:28).

Such is the way of Brother Lawrence of the Resurrection. For three centuries his simple wisdom has crossed denominational boundaries and theological differences to inspire spiritual seekers throughout the world. The universality of his appeal is extraordinary, but it is due in large part to the very ordinariness he taught. God is available in ordinary life, in the commonest places and most mundane activities. The practice of God's presence can be as simple as a little interior glance, as plain as a bare desire.

In the early years of publication of Brother Lawrence's teachings, during and after the Quietist controversy, his simple, no-nonsense approach was refreshing and reassuring to Roman Catholics and Protestants alike. It continues to be so today, especially in an American milieu of pop psycho-spirituality. Here is down-to-earth wisdom, a timeless mysticism without frills, a joyful spirituality without hype.

This faithfully translated new edition is the most complete and comprehensive text on Brother Lawrence available. It is a scholarly work, painstakingly researched and edited, carefully annotated and cross-referenced. Here is all the pertinent material, including some for the first time in English. Each section is preceded by a critical and reflective Introductory Note. Taken together, these factors assure the reader of the best possible appreciation of Brother Lawrence's practice, life experience, and personality.

In addition, the text provides a valuable location of Brother Lawrence within his historical context. The stream of spiritual history that fed Brother Lawrence's spirituality is carefully referenced, from the headwaters of the Gospel through his formative predecessors (including Saint Teresa of Avila and Saint John of the Cross), to his own experience within the Carmelite monastery of Paris, to his influence upon succeeding generations and his relevance for our time.

Especially illuminating is the inclusion of material pertaining to the Quietist turbulence and the Fénelon-Bossuet controversy. These waves of accusation and defense, in stark dissonance with Brother Lawrence's own style, raise fascinating theological questions about hope and self-interest in the spiritual life.

Readers will also have the opportunity to grapple with theological assumptions and language that were common in Brother Lawrence's time but can be problematic in our own. He speaks, for example, of the necessity of abandoning creatures, even scorning them. But he also tells us we must love our friends. He says God gives us illnesses and suffering as graces for our salvation. But he also maintains God always wants to aid the afflicted and change suffering into sweetness. Fénelon called Brother Lawrence uneducated, but a profound theological precision is to be found beneath the surface of Brother Lawrence's words. Dive deeply into his exquisite theology of suffering and grace, for example; there are treasures to be found there.

Fénelon also called Brother Lawrence "rough by nature but delicate (or sensitive) in grace." This combination can be seen in Brother Lawrence's own words. There is a rough, even tough quality in his single-minded dedication to the practice of the presence of God. There is no time to waste, either in distraction or in regrets. There is no time for fear or worry, no place for despair. There is hardly even time for thinking. In every present moment we must get on with living in the direct, immediate love of God. Nothing is more important than this, nothing more worthy of our serious intent. But there is also honest humility and gentle compassion in Brother Lawrence. He truly understands the struggles we go through, for he has experienced them himself. He gracefully brings a lightness to our difficulties, along with a bright humor and exuberance clearly born of his direct experience of God's goodness.

Brother Lawrence maintains that the practice of the presence of God is both simple and easy. Americans may agree that it is simple, but most of us will not find it so easy. We will tend, as with everything, to look at it as something to achieve. We will see it in terms of success or failure. With this view we will find ourselves failures and the practice nearly impossible. We need to try to look at it in Brother Lawrence's way, as an endeavor requiring our sincere desire and earnest dedication, but wholly dependent upon God's grace. Then, even in our failures, we come back to God's presence, to God's mercy. With Brother Lawrence, we can say to God, "It's up to you."

Gerald G. May, M.D.

A surviving portion of Brother Lawrence's monastery in Paris, now part of the Institut Catholique (Photographer unknown.)

Foreword to the French Edition

The enclosure at 21 Rue d'Assas in the heart of Paris's sixth ward [arrondissement] is indeed a most historic place. The Institut Catholique, set up within these walls in 1895, has experienced a rich yet stormy history that extends into the present. Among its professors and illustrious guests were Lacordaire, Ozanam, Branly, Rousselot, Teilhard de Chardin, Duchesne, and Dubarle, to speak only of the departed. Its heritage, however, is deeply rooted in a history of sanctity and heroism. The [Discalced] Carmelite friars established their foundation here in 1611; the bishops and priests imprisoned here were massacred on September 2, 1792; Mother [Camille] de Soyecourt, prioress of the [Discalced] Carmelite nuns, bought back the buildings after the French Revolution.

To commemorate these ancestors here, whether famous or obscure, is to rediscover something of a religious tradition still carried on in the spiritual exercises and meditations of the future priests of the present seminary, the former Carmelite monastery.

The Church of Saint Joseph and its crypt, the corridors and cells, the storerooms and attic, and especially the garden, remain today as they were when first constructed at the beginning of the seventeenth century by Marie de Médicis, whose express wish was to to establish a Discalced Carmelite monastery here. Living each day in this age-old atmosphere of silence and spiritual meditation allows us to better appreciate the life and writings of Brother Lawrence of the Resurrection, one of the first friars.

Lawrence, the man from Lorraine who came to Paris, soldier turned lay brother, the monastery cook and sandalmaker, was a spiritual guide widely recognized and sought after during his lifetime. We can easily picture him as he wandered through the vaulted corridors and hallways, the refectory (still intact), the recently restored cloister, the arcades, and the fragrant garden. We see him in the ordinary comings and goings of everyday life, in the church and

xiii

the Fathers' chapels on the second floor, near the chapter room, the scriptorium and the library. A brown-robed presence, the presence of a religious soul in constant search of the Presence of God, who revealed to many others the "practice" of this presence: a simple, demanding, radiant method that informed the life of one of the sons of Saints Teresa of Avila and John of the Cross, and a method lived out "among the pots and pans," despite the many cares of a lay brother in a monastery numbering more than one hundred priests and brothers.

"In my opinion, the practice of the presence of God is the essence of the spiritual life, and it seems to me that when practiced properly, you become spiritual in no time." He experienced intimacy with God, a dark night of faith that lasted several years, the trial of a deteriorating body toward the end of his life, but also the comforting joy of an inner peace that finds its center and resting place in the presence of God. Lawrence's simple words, collected immediately after his death, evoked numerous echoes even in the Protestant, Anglo-Saxon world.

This new edition will certainly find a large audience among twentieth century men and women who are overburdened, tired, distracted from what is essential, yet desirous, perhaps without realizing it, of peace, silence, fraternal communion, spiritual simplicity, and the presence of God.

"Everyone is capable of these intimate conversations with God, some more, some less, and God knows what we can do." This is a simple, humble way to God, and one we can rely on forever.

Paul Guiberteau

Translator's Preface

Long before I ever thought of becoming a Discalced Carmelite friar, I was touched by Brother Lawrence of the Resurrection. I read his *Conversations* years ago and was deeply struck by his grace of conversion—his insight that God's providence and power would bring the dead tree back to life. I found his simple doctrine of the practice of the Presence of God truly profound. It should be no surprise, then, that I considered the request to translate Father Conrad De Meester's critical edition of the *Writings and Conversations* of Brother Lawrence a grace and privilege.

I met Father Conrad two years ago, and we discussed the text he had prepared for the third centenary of the death of Brother Lawrence. His devotion to Brother Lawrence is evident from the thoroughness of his edition. Several features are significant: He has written a fine general introduction for the book, which includes a biographical sketch, a description of the writings, and a discussion of the various editions (in several languages) and their impact. The main section of the book includes all the writings by Brother Lawrence himself, and those about him by his biographer, Joseph de Beaufort. There are also three valuable appendices. The first describes the Discalced Carmelite monastery and province of Paris during Brother Lawrence's lifetime. The second is a letter by Beaufort defending Lawrence against the charge of Quietism, presented here in English for the first time. The third appendix contains all the references made to Brother Lawrence in the Fénelon-Bossuet controversy, which had a lasting impact on French spirituality and on Lawrence's reputation among Catholics and Protestants alike. Finally, for this American edition we have added a brief bibliography of related works in English.

My own translation is an attempt to capture Brother Lawrence's spirit and style, and to convey them in idiomatic American English. Attention was given to the different literary genres:

eulogy, letters, maxims, and so on. I have translated certain terms into more customary Carmelite language: "friar" rather than "monk," for example, or "mental prayer" rather than "meditation" for the hours of silent personal prayer practiced in our monasteries. Several Discalced Carmelite brothers suggested "lay brother" as the least problematic translation for "frère convers" (distinguished from those in the community of Carmelite friars who were also priests).

Even though Father Conrad's edition of the 17th century texts is done in contemporary French, I found it necessary to refashion much of the sentence structure in the individual paragraphs to make the English version clearer and easier to read. Some French terms posed a particular challenge. For example, in 17th century French ecclesiastical circles the honorific title *Monseigneur* was commonly used to address bishops and cardinals rather than clergy of lower rank; accordingly, I have used "Your Excellency" rather than the somewhat misleading *Monsignor* where the context makes it appropriate (see especially Appendix III). More significantly, I have translated the expression *regard interieur* as "awareness" rather than "inner gaze," because this, I believe, is what Brother Lawrence meant by it.

Finally, I want to thank Father Daniel, O.C.D. (of the Paris Province of Discalced Carmelites), Steven Payne, O.C.D, Robert Stefanotti, O.Carm., Professor Anne D. Cordero, Ph.D., and Jude Langsam, O.C.D.S., for their invaluable assistance.

Salvatore Sciurba, O.C.D.

General Introduction

*For the third centenary of
the death of Brother Lawrence (1691–1991)*

On February 12, 1691, Brother Lawrence of the Resurrection died at the Discalced Carmelite Monastery, Rue Vaugirard, in Paris—the same house where, on September 2, 1792, a century later, two bishops and twelve priests were put to death during the furor of the French Revolution. At present, this house is part of the Institut Catholique of Paris.

Lawrence of the Resurrection, cook and sandalmaker, lived an intense experience of God at the service of "pure" love, an ideal at the forefront of the study of mysticism and theological discussion at the time. What happened after his death is no less astonishing! Fénelon and Bossuet, in their well-known and bitter quarrel, would often discuss questions taken from the writings and conversations of Brother Lawrence, and Protestant publishers, interested witnesses of the debate, diffused his writings widely.

This is why Lawrence of the Resurrection was practically forgotten in his own country until the time of Pierre Pourrat[1] and the perceptive Henri Bremond (who described this Brother as one of the most outstanding mystics),[2] although Lawrence was translated and retranslated abroad. In Brother Lawrence's own country people are still surprised to see his *Practice of the Presence of God* described as "famous throughout the world" by a specialist like Father Titus Brandsma,[3] or to read in the writings of Aldous Huxley himself that Lawrence "has enjoyed a kind of celebrity in circles otherwise completely uninterested in mental prayer or spiritual exercises."[4]

Brother Lawrence has become a friend of the many seekers of God through the depth of his experience, his common sense, and his engaging disposition, and therefore deserves renewed and more serious attention.

Biographical Sketch

We will rapidly recount Brother Lawrence's life, leaving the development of his inner journey for another place.[5]

His given name was Nicolas Herman and, unfortunately, we have few details of his youth. Nicolas was born in 1614 at Hériménil,[6] a small village near Lunéville in Lorraine. He learned Christian principles from his parents Dominic and Louise, who were "very fine people" (EL 7). But the biographer's compliment extended only to their human and religious qualities and not to their material well-being, because Nicolas, who would give evidence of sound intelligence, apparently did not have the opportunity to study.

We do not know whether Nicolas had brothers or sisters, how he spent his childhood, or what his academic training and first employment might have been.

At the age of eighteen, a sudden, cosmic intuition of the grandeur and presence of God grasped him profoundly (CN 1). It was a silent call of the divine mystery and a first conversion.

Nonetheless Nicolas did not turn toward religious life but chose instead "military service" (EL 8) during this troubled period of the terribly destructive Thirty Years' War. At one point Nicolas Herman was arrested by "German" troops. Suspected of being a spy, he was threatened with death, though he was able to establish his innocence. He rejoined the Lorraine troops but was wounded during the siege of Rambervillers (1635). Nicolas then returned to his parents' home (EL 8-9).

We wonder if he, as a soldier, participated in one way or another in the lootings often accompanied by the atrocious, cruel violence so characteristic of the Thirty Years' War. He would later deplore the "disorders of his youth" (EL 12) and the "sins of his past life" (EL 21), "determined to rectify his past conduct" (EL 10).

He searched intensely. In any event, we can imagine an inner struggle before he decided to try the eremetical life and joined a gentleman living in solitude (EL 13-15). He was not mature enough, however, for this kind of life, which he abandoned. We can most likely situate his stay in Paris as the "valet" of M. de Fieubet (CN 2) after his attempt at the hermit life.

At the age of twenty-six he made a serious decision. In mid-June of 1640,[7] he entered the Order of Discalced Carmelites on the Rue Vaugirard[8] in Paris, as a lay brother. In mid-August Nicolas Herman received the brown Carmelite habit and took the religious name of Lawrence (perhaps the patron saint of his village)[9] completing it with the title "of the Resurrection," a mystery he admirably lived in the sight of the living God and his Christ.

During the novitiate the lay brothers attended certain formation classes with the young clerics, complemented by other classes adapted to their tasks and possible future duties.[10] The new Brother Lawrence of the Resurrection admitted he was disappointed even to the point of reproaching the Lord, "You have tricked me!" He entered fearing "they would skin him alive" for his awkwardness and faults—as he said in his own unpolished, simple language,[11] often seasoned with humor—but fortunately for himself and his brothers he "experienced only satisfaction" (CN 3).

Nonetheless he did enter into a dark night that would continue a number of years, the last four of which were the most harsh.[12] He feared he would be lost, for he had the impression, as he said, that "I was damning myself, that there was no salvation for me at all." On one hand, he experienced God intimately, but on the other, his desire to please God in everything was the source of his distress. "The fear that I had not given myself to God as I desired, my sins always present before my eyes, and the great graces God gave me were the sum and substance of all my woes." In this conflict he used only one insignificant, yet at the same time powerful, weapon: "It seemed to me that creatures, reason, and even God himself were against me, and that faith alone was on my side." His impressive testimony, taken from a personal letter (L 2), also sketches the outcome: "Once I accepted the fact I might spend the rest of my life in this troubled state of mind...I found myself changed all at once. And my soul, up to that time in turmoil, now experienced a profound inner peace, as if it were in its center and resting place." How frequently and intensely he dwelt there! Lawrence's entire method can be summed up in the return to the presence of God, whose consoling love he often experienced.

We are getting ahead of our story, however. The two years of his novitiate completed, this young brother made his solemn profession of vows on August 14, 1642, at the age of twenty-eight. Louis de Sainte-Thérèse,[13] his prior, summed up the lay brother's vocation as one of "prayer and manual work." Following his profession, Lawrence was the cook for the Parisian community for "fifteen years" (CN 18). Some years this community numbered about one hundred friars,[14] including many young men in formation.[15]

More and more, however, Lawrence suffered from "a kind of sciatic gout that made him limp" (EL 50). This may have been the result of the wound he received on the battlefield. The kitchen became too difficult a task for someone physically handicapped, so they entrusted him with an assignment where he could sit, the sandal shop (CN 19). There he repaired the two hundred sandals of the Discalced Carmelites.

But the brother sandalmaker was also entrusted with other assignments, for example, buying the wine. This called for a long journey to Auvergne in 1665, one that might have taken three weeks to cover the eight hundred-some kilometers round-trip, thus allowing him to establish all sorts of contacts. In 1666, he would make a six hundred kilometer round-trip to Bourgogne by river, so difficult for him that this poor brother, "crippled in one leg, could only get about on the boat by rolling over the barrels" (CN 17).

These were not his only opportunities to make contacts. There were the workers who came to the monastery, the beggars at the door, and the visitors to both the parlors and the church. The lay brothers had to go out for all sorts of errands, often to beg money for the living expenses of the community, which was composed largely of young friars in formation.[16] And his own confreres certainly benefited from the advice and example of this silent witness to the presence of God.

Gradually, the influence of the humble brother sandalmaker grew, and not only among the poor he helped and advised (EL 49). His biographer, who visited him regularly from 1666, made known the esteem that "many learned people, religious, and ecclesiastics had for him" (EL 39). Father Goujet of Paris may have exaggerated when he presented Brother Lawrence as venerated by "all Paris."[17] Nonetheless, it is true that many people, and not only the least influential, greatly appreciated the conversation of this humble brother, so anchored in God. His biographer gave the example of "an outstanding bishop of France" who had several conversations with Lawrence.[18]

Fénelon, another visitor, deserves special note. He went to see Lawrence shortly before he died, and the memory of the meeting was still vivid ten years later. "The words of the saints themselves," he wrote, "are often very different from the discourse of those who tried to describe them. Saint Catherine of Genoa was prodigious in love. Brother Lawrence was rough by nature but delicate in grace. This mixture was appealing, and revealed God present in him. I saw him, and there is a place in the book where the author, without mentioning me by name, briefly related a fine conversation I had with him on death, and even though he was very sick, he remained very happy."[19] And here is Fénelon's reply to Bossuet: "You can always learn by studying God's action on experienced though uneducated souls. Could we not have learned the practice of the presence of God by conversing with Brother Lawrence, for example?"[20]

Though Brother Lawrence had something to say to the learned, "he hid nothing from the little ones and the most simple" (EL 37)! When it came to the practice of the presence of God, "he counseled all his friends to apply themselves to it with all the care and fidelity possible" (EL 31).

His biographer has left us a portrait of his social virtues. "Brother Lawrence's virtue never made him harsh. He was open, eliciting confidence, letting you feel you could tell him anything, and that you had found a friend. For his part, once he knew who he was dealing with, he spoke freely and showed great goodness. What he said was simple, yet always appropriate, and made good sense. Once you got past his rough exterior you discovered unusual wisdom, a freedom beyond the reach of the ordinary lay brother, an insight that extended far beyond what you would expect" (W 3). He had "the best heart in the world. His fine countenance, his human, affable air, his simple, modest manner won him the esteem and good will of all who saw him. The more closely you looked, the more you discovered in him a depth of integrity and piety rarely found elsewhere.... He was not one of those inflexible people who consider sanctity incompatible with ordinary manners. He associated with everyone and never put on airs, acting kindly towards his brothers and friends without wanting to be conspicuous" (EL 35).

Lawrence possessed a certain intellectual training. He sometimes spoke of the books he had read or examined.[21] He had the opportunity to hear many fine sermons in the monastery church or those of Paris (EL 43). And then there were his confreres and the visiting experts! Lawrence was nourished by the spirit of holy Mother Saint Teresa of Avila whose *Way of Perfection* was read in the refectory every year. The Madre's statement that "the Lord walks among the pots and pans" must have pleased the brother cook.[22] Judging from his writings, he must have also have found joy in reading Saint John of the Cross, whose works were remarkably well translated by Cyprian of the Nativity, one of his confreres.[23] Lawrence certainly read and heard explained the exhortations of the Venerable John of Jesus and Mary (of Calahorra, Spain), the official teacher, you might say, of the Discalced Carmelite Order in the seventeenth century.[24] The counsels of John of Jesus and Mary (very fervent but rather detailed, and couched in lengthy vocal prayers) could not have pleased Brother Lawrence for long, because his simple life was centered on the presence of God, infinitely admired, faithfully sought after, and sweetly experienced.[25]

If Lawrence spoke, he was more often silent. The lay brothers lived in the shadows, in the already profound silence of Carmel. Juridically, they occupied the last place in the house, for even the cleric novices ranked ahead of them. Except for rare occasions, they did not attend the choral Office but instead recited a certain number of "Our Fathers," the admirable prayer! In the morning they served the priests' masses. Most days, because of their duties, they could not make the morning or evening hours of silent prayer in common but, according to the instructions of the prior, made their prayer at other times, very often at night.[26] But Lawrence, and we will read this many times, was accustomed to living constantly in the presence of God, praying without respite, in all circumstances. His heart had become "prayerified."

For more than fifty years the always obliging good-heartedness of Lawrence—who lived the depth of a contemplation that was the source of the wisdom of his counsels—delighted and inspired the friars of the monastery on the Rue Vaugirard.

His physical sufferings increased, however. The sciatic gout that caused his limping tormented him for about twenty-five years and degenerated into an ulcer of the leg, leaving him in intense pain (EL 50). He was ill three times during the last years of his life. When he recovered the first time he said to the physician: "Doctor, your remedies have worked too well for me. You have only delayed my happiness!" (EL 51). He anxiously awaited the glorious Encounter. Three weeks before he died he wrote "Goodbye, I hope to see him soon" (L 16). And six days before the end: "I hope for the merciful grace of seeing him in a few days" (L 16).

Lucid up to the last moments, Brother Lawrence of the Resurrection died on February 12, 1691, at the age of seventy-seven.

Writings and Conversations

We will now consider what remains of Brother Lawrence's work. First, there is a precious collection of sixteen *Lettres* [Letters] (L). The circulation of a copy of one of the letters provoked interest, and so his biographer took the trouble to gather all the available correspondence (EL 2). Lawrence wrote an interesting personal letter to a religious priest, others to a Carmelite nun, some others to one or more lay people, and the last four to a Blessed Sacrament nun.[27]

Along with the letters, also transcribed was "a manuscript entitled *Maximes spirituelles ou Moyens pour acquérir la présence de Dieu* [Spiritual maxims, or the means to attain the presence of God]" (EL 2), a little work on the search for God in everyday life (SM).[28]

His biographer, who had frequent contacts with Brother Lawrence over a period of thirty-five years, provided a summary of the first four *Entretiens* [Conversations] (CN)[29] along with the comforting reassurance: "Brother Lawrence will speak for himself. I will give you his own words taken from the conversations I wrote down as soon as I had left him" (W 2).

His biographer also presented a personal work: *Pratique de l'exercice de la présence de Dieu tirée des Lettres du Frère Laurent* [Practice of the presence of God taken from the letters of Brother Lawrence].

Although the texts he included are already found in the letters, dispersed throughout in various places,[30] this little work is a summary of our mystic's thought, and for this reason we have included it in this edition.

Finally, there are two biographical sketches that, in spite of certain repetitions, complement each other harmoniously: the *Éloge* [Eulogy] (EL), which the reader will find placed before Lawrence's own texts, and Lawrence's *Moeurs* [Ways] (W), at the end of the volume. The biographer successfully enriched his personal memories with numerous pieces of information.[31]

The controversy regarding Fénelon's book *Maxims of the Saints* would later prompt Brother Lawrence's biographer to publish a brochure intended to safeguard him from all suspicion of the Quietist error. Though not especially useful in terms of providing a better, more detailed knowledge of our mystic, the text is given nonetheless as an appendix.[32]

Various French Editions

We will now consider in some detail the various French editions of Lawrence's writings and conversations, up to the present.

First Edition

By the first edition we mean two little volumes, dated 1692 and 1694, the two-part work of an anonymous biographer in two parts. The first is: "*Maximes spirituelles fort utiles aux âmes pieuses, pour acquérir la presence de Dieu. Recueillies de quelques Manuscrits du Frère Laurent de la Résurrection, Religieux Convers des Carmes Déchaussés. Avec l'abrégé de la Vie de l'Auteur et quelques Lettres qu'il a écrites à des personnes de piété* [Spiritual maxims most useful for pious souls to attain the presence of God. Collected from some manuscripts of Brother Lawrence of the Resurrection, Discalced Carmelite lay brother. With an abridged life of the author and some of his letters to persons of piety], published in Paris by Edmé Couterot, Rue Saint-Jacques, Bon Pasteur, 1692, with approbation and permission."[33] This duodecimo volume contains 6 + 182 pages.

The second is: *"Les Mœurs et Entretiens du Frère Laurent de la Résurrection, Religieux Carme Déchaussé. Avec la Pratique de l'Exercise de la présence de Dieu, tirée de ses Lettres* [The ways and conversations of Brother Lawrence of the Resurrection, Discalced Carmelite lay brother. With the practice of the presence of God, taken from his letters], published at Chaalons, by Jacques Seneuze, His Excellency's Printer and Bookseller, 1694, with permission and privilege." This duodecimo volume contains 92 pages. In the "permission" (approbation) of the book, Louis-Antoine (de Noailles), bishop of Châlons-sur-Marne, wrote on November 17, 1693: "We recommend the reading of it to all persons who desire to attain true piety, certain that the example and maxims of this faithful servant of God will benefit them greatly" (p. 91). Convinced that some of his condemned mystical theses were scarcely different from those of Brother Lawrence, Fénelon soon remembered the favorable approbation of de Noailles, now archbishop of Paris and associate of Bossuet in the bitter debate against the archbishop of Cambrai.

Second Edition

The mystical debate between Fénelon and Bossuet (supported by de Noailles and Godet des Marais, bishop of Chartres) led to the unfortunate condemnation of Fénelon's book, *Maxims of the Saints,* on March 12, 1699.[34] Thus the tragic controversy came to an end. "In the area of spirituality," however, "its consequences would be felt for a long time to come, and in some respects may still affect us," wrote Louis Cognet in 1958.[35] Henceforth "almost all public expressions of mystical tendencies were declared impossible," wrote Jacques Le Brun, and "as always happens in a case like this, there arose a veritable antiquietist obsession in the Catholic Church."[36]

This immense upheaval had profound consequences in the Protestant world. De Noailles quoted "the Holland gazettes"[37] often mentioned in the correspondence relative to Quietism. This controversy may explain why Lawrence was forgotten in France—he was used as evidence by the losing party, wrongly associated with Quietism, and upheld by the Protestants. Yet it is to Fénelon, and obviously to his own intrinsic worth, that our Brother owes his posthumous international influence, of which we will speak later.

We have not strayed from the history of Lawrence's French editions. For it was in this climate, and outside France, that the second appeared, in a collection with the writings of Madame Guyon, whose personal integrity and mystical authenticity Fénelon defended while at the same time recognizing the lacunae in her expressions. Eight years after his death, then, Lawrence's work had its second edition, in *"Recueil de divers Traités de théologie mystique, qui entrent dans la Célèbre Dispute du Quiétisme qui s'agite présentement en France. Contenant I. Le Moyen court et très facile de faire Oraison. II. L'Explication du Cantique des Cantiques. Tous deux par Madame Guyon. III. L'Éloge, les Maximes spirituelles et quelques Lettres du Fr. Laurent de la Résurrection. IV. Les Mœurs et Entretiens du même Fr. Laurent et sa Pratique de l'exercice de la présence de Dieu. Avec une Préface où l'on voit beaucoup de particularités de la vie de Madame Guyon.* [A collection of various treatises of mystical theology that enter into the famous dispute of Quietism currently stirring in France. Containing: I. The short, easy way to make mental prayer. II. Explanation of the Canticle of Canticles. Both by Madame Guyon. III. The eulogy, the spiritual maxims and some letters of Brother Lawrence of the Resurrection. IV. The ways and conversations of the same Brother Lawrence and his practice of the presence of God. With a preface where one finds many similarities with the life of Madame Guyon.] Published in Cologne by Jean de la Pierre, 1699." The texts of Brother Lawrence are found in this duodecimo volume on pages 399 to 493.

The publisher still remains anonymous. It was not Pierre Poiret, even though he did promote this edition with his advice.[38] The name of the publisher is fictitious; there was no "Jean de la Pierre" in Cologne. This edition came from Holland[39] and was most likely published by Henri Wetstein in Amsterdam.[40]

Third Edition

Eleven years later, and once again abroad, the third edition of Brother Lawrence's work made its appearance: *"La Théologie de la Présence de Dieu, contenant la Vie, les Mœurs, les Entretiens, la Pratique et les Lettres du Frère Laurent de la Résurrection. Avec un Traité de l'importance et des avantages de la pratique de la Présence de Dieu, qu'on appuye de témoignages divins et humains* [The theology of the presence of God, containing the life, the ways, the conversations, the practice, and the letters of Brother Lawrence of the Resurrection. With a treatise on the importance and the advantages of the practice of the presence of God, upheld by divine and human witnesses]. Published in Cologne, by Jean de la Pierre, 1710. With approbation and permissions." This duodecimo volume contains 14 + 344 pages. The "treatise" mentioned in the title follows the texts of Brother Lawrence and covers almost half the book (pp. 179–344), and is signed P.P. (no doubt Pierre Poiret). "Brother Lawrence's method, although he is unschooled, is among the most excellent you can find because of its simplicity and its ease, its great soundness, and because it touches your heart."[41] It is undoubtedly Pierre Poiret himself who prepared the entire third edition, including the Publisher's Foreword, thereby performing a critical task rarely undertaken by a publisher.[42]

Fourth Edition

The prestige of the Protestant minister Pierre Poiret (1646–1719), very open to Catholicism and publisher of many authors including Brother Lawrence, had a great deal to do with the international influence Lawrence exerted through the German and English translations. However, it took more than two centuries before a new French edition was published in 1924, once again due to our Protestant brethren. We are referring to *"La Pratique de la Présence de Dieu, comprenant les 'Entretiens,' les 'Maximes Spirituelles' et les 'Lettres' du Frère Laurent, carme déchaussé (1611 [sic]–1691). Première réédition complète reproduite intégralment d'après les textes originaux de la Bibliothèque Nationale* [The practice of the presence of God, including the "Conversations," the "Spiritual Maxims," and the "Letters" of Brother Lawrence, Discalced Carmelite (1611 [sic]–1691). Newly reproduced in their entirety from the original[43] texts taken from the Bibliotheque Nationale]," Paris, Fischbacher Bookstore and the Christian Society of Friends (Quakers), 1924, 157 pages.[44]

We find this typical passage in the "Note to the Reader" (pp. 7–8): "If the works of Brother Lawrence have remained unknown in France, they have long had, nonetheless, a wide circulation in England. Many editions have been published, and it is not going too far to say that the *Practice of the Presence of God,* as it is generally known, is a book of piety almost as well known as the *Imitation of Christ* or the *Little Flowers of Saint Francis.* We have no idea why this work has remained so little known in France, but, aware of the spiritual help many Christians have found in this profoundly mystical and eminently practical work, we are convinced we are doing the right thing in trying to make better known to his own compatriots all that this humble, faithful servant of Jesus Christ left us. He belongs neither to Catholicism nor to Protestantism, but to all those who, regardless of their religious affiliation, try to make Jesus King in their daily life."

Fifth Edition

The following edition, published in Belgium, is due to a great lay friend of Carmel, Louis Van den Bossche: "Fr. Laurent de la Résurrection, Convers Carme déchaussé (†1691), *La Pratique de la présence de Dieu* [Brother Lawrence of the Resurrection, Discalced Carmelite lay brother (†1691), *Practice of the Presence of God*]. New edition, with preface and notes by Louis Van den Bossche." Desclee De Brouwer and Co., 1934, 232 pages.[45]

Sixth Edition

After the Second World War, Father François de Sainte-Marie, who had already expressed his regret that his Parisian confrere was "so little known,"[46] included him in his "La Vigne du Carmel" [Vine of Carmel] series: "*L'Expérience de la présence de Dieu* [The experience of the presence of God], by Brother Lawrence of the Resurrection. Text established by S. M. Boucheraux and presented by Rev. Fr. François de Sainte-Marie," Paris, Édition du Seuil, 1948, 159 pages.

Our Edition and Its Features

The third centenary of the death of Brother Lawrence provides the occasion for this new edition, and it is certainly most appropriate given the impact this humble Brother has had for centuries. We researched whether there might be *other* existing manuscripts besides those the first biographer published, and if the *originals* he used for his work could be tracked down. We were not able to go beyond the first printed texts.[47] Our investigations and research at the Carmelite and Parisian archives (Bibliothèque nationale, bibliothèque de l'Arsenal, bibliothèque Mazarine, Archives nationales, bibliothèque Sainte-Geneviève, bibliothèque de l'Université de Paris, Bibliothèque historique de la Ville de Paris) were in vain.[48] The upheavals that the libraries and religious archives of France underwent are well known. The first biographer himself tells us he could find only some "fragments," leading him to regret the loss of the rest of the writings, sometimes created on the spur of the moment, but unfortunately "often torn up then and there" (EL 42).

We have tried to arrange everything in the best possible order in accord with the historical and spiritual context. Here is the order we have adopted: the *Eulogy* (this is the first biographical sketch), the *Spiritual Maxims,* the *Letters,* the *Conversations,* the *Practice of the Presence of God,* and the *Ways* (the second biographical sketch).

Each section has its introductory note, and three appendices complete our edition. Appendix I offers a brief historical sketch and a plan of the monastery on the Rue Vaugirard where Brother Lawrence lived. Appendix II presents the *Letter to Msgr. M. de ...,* in which the biographer defends Lawrence from all suspicion of Quietism, a difficult text to find today, and one never republished. Appendix III gives the passages dealing with Brother Lawrence in the polemic texts of Fénelon, Bossuet and de Noailles.

We have updated the spelling, the punctuation, the sentence structure, and the use of capital letters. We have also numbered certain paragraphs and added critical and explanatory notes.

Joseph De Beaufort,
The Anonymous Biographer-Editor

It is not until the third edition of 1710 that we discover the name of the original biographer-editor, at least for the second book, the *Ways*. Pierre Poiret informs us: "We do not know to whom we owe the edition of the first [book of *Spiritual Maxims*] but for the second we do know that it was Joseph de Beaufort, vicar of the bishop of Châlons, who wrote the *Ways* of Brother Lawrence, and to whom we most likely also owe the rest." [49] This is what the tradition has constantly affirmed.

In Bossuet's *Correspondance* and in that of Fénelon, we find the proof of Beaufort's literary authorship affirmed by Poiret. Recall the *Letter to Msgr. M. de* ... (see Appendix II). The title continues: ...*to defend the Book of the Ways and the Conversations of Brother Lawrence of the Resurrection, Discalced Carmelite, printed in Châlons in 1694, by the author of the book, a priest of the diocese of Paris.*

The author of this *Letter*, and therefore also of the *Ways*, is indeed Joseph de Beaufort. On October 14, 1697, more than a month before the publication of the *Letter*,[50] Bossuet wrote to his nephew in Rome: "Remember Brother Lawrence, whose case is before the bishop of Paris [de Noailles]. You will perhaps receive a letter on the subject by this ordinary, under the name of Joseph de Beaufort. It is well written and you can circulate it."

The testimony of Fénelon, the archbishop of Cambrai, is even stronger. On November 19, 1697, he wrote to Father de Chanterac, his defender in Rome: "You will have seen a letter from Joseph de Beaufort that the bishop of Meaux [Bossuet] had him write, and which they sent to Rome to defend Brother Lawrence of the Resurrection, and to show that he is not in conformity with my book. The same de Beaufort wrote me a letter of apology on this subject that I am sending to you." [51] On another occasion Fénelon had written[52] to de Noailles about the *Ways* of Brother Lawrence, "Let's get to the book done at your command, before your eyes, in your house,[53] by your vicar who enjoyed your confidence for years," another allusion to Joseph de Beaufort, "the confessor and counselor" [54] of the former bishop of Châlons-sur-Marne, who became archbishop of

Paris in 1695. It is true that the testimonies cited only prove Beaufort's authorship in regard to the *Ways,* the only one of the two books that Fénelon continuously quoted.[55] We can nonetheless accept Pierre Poiret's opinion that we "owe the rest to Beaufort" because eminent specialists also support this tradition.[56] As far as we know, no other authorship has been attributed to the *Spiritual Maxims,* and it is highly unlikely that two different biographers (apparently ecclesiastics who were not Carmelites) would have been so impressed by this lay brother that they would both have written his life story. In addition, the style and punctuation of the two sketches are similar. The second narrative takes up the account of Lawrence's illness and death almost literally without any reference to the first of the two works, and the two works complement each other perfectly. There can be no doubt that Joseph de Beaufort is the one author of both works.

The biographical dictionaries tell us nothing about this intelligent, somewhat self-effacing man who preferred second place in spite of his rank. We must put together carefully the little stones we have collected to form a biographical mosaic. Joseph de Beaufort had his first conversations with Lawrence in 1666–1667. He was a friend of Carmel. During the summer of 1663, we find him at the Discalced Carmelite monastery in Nevers, making a retreat with a younger brother, also a priest, whom he wanted to lead back to a more intense spiritual life. Eustache, 26 years old, was abbot of the Cistercians of Sept-Fons, near Moulins, and had until then led an easygoing life, rather taken up by worldly cares. He experienced a conversion during the retreat with his older brother Joseph, and later became the holy reformer of his abbey, which would then greatly flourish.

Beaufort's family came from Paris. Joseph must have been born around 1635. His father became the "king's secretary" and exercised this office as the gentleman of the duke of Noailles, father of Louis-Antoine.[57] That explains the close bond between Joseph and Louis-Antoine. De Noailles, who became bishop of Châlons-sur-Marne in 1680, chose Joseph, who was already in his service, as his trusted collaborator. In the letter of appointment written on December 12, 1690, we read: "We name as vicar general Msgr. Joseph de Beaufort, priest of Paris, licensed *in utroque jure* [in civil and canon law], canon and archdeacon of our cathedral."[58] When de Noailles became archbishop of Paris in 1695, Joseph followed him as vicar general.[59] It was not only because of his work on Brother Lawrence that Beaufort's name occasionally appeared in the correspondence of Fénelon, longtime friend of de Noailles. It was in the presence of Beaufort himself, confidant and one of the archbishop's theologians, that Fénelon had read to de Noailles the manuscript of his book, *Explanation of the Maxims of the Saints*, stating its merits, before its condemnation.[60]

Brother Lawrence's International Influence

We now turn to the consideration of Brother Lawrence's extraordinary impact outside of France.

German-speaking Countries

Intrigued by the Bossuet-Fénelon controversy and condemnation of 1699, the Protestants—more precisely those adhering to the "pietist" movement—were anxious to translate and diffuse Fénelon and his favorite authors. That is why, as early as 1701, Brother Lawrence (together with Madame Guyon) was completely translated into German,[61] with a preface by the famous Gottfried Arnold.[62] The book was republished in 1706.[63] In 1714 an entirely new translation of Brother Lawrence appeared, based on the third French edition, that of Pierre Poiret.[64] This was the beginning of a long series of German translations that continues to the present.

Besides the unabridged translations, biographies of the lay brother soon appeared in German. Gottfried Arnold had already written a biography in 1701.[65] In 1717, Johann Heinrich Reitz followed his example.[66] But it was especially the great spiritual master Gerhard Tersteegen—the impression he made on Kierkegaard is well known, and Walter Nigg considered him to be a model *par excellence* of the "Protestant saint"—who, very open to the Catholic spiritual masters, played a major role in the diffusion of Brother Lawrence's thought in Germany and the Low Countries during the eighteenth and nineteenth centuries.[67] Lawrence exerted a "decisive influence" on Tersteegen regarding the discovery of the Presence of God.[68] In Tersteegen's "selected biographies" he devoted a very long chapter to the lay brother who had traced the way of salvation "in a clearer, shorter manner than a doctor in theology could have done, showing by his example that not only clerics and religious, but each one of us, no matter what our state of life, can live in the presence of God."[69]

English-speaking Countries

Brother Lawrence was not immediately translated into English; nonetheless the success he would later enjoy was even greater. Jean Orcibal wrote that this "humble lay brother, most advanced in the mystical ways,"[70] benefited from the climate created by the Archbishop of Cambrai in England: "We are right in concluding, along with the perceptive Alexander Knox, that during the 100 years following his death, no Catholic was more popular in a Protestant country than Fénelon. His spiritual influence was immense, but we must not exclude those who supported him, whether it is a question of friends or disciples, such as Brother Lawrence, Madame Guyon, P. Poiret, Ramsey, and mystics of other schools."[71]

Brother Lawrence, soon known in the Anglican Church through the original French versions of his texts, was at last translated into English in 1724 by John Heylin,[72] with the help of Dr. George Cheyne and William Law,[73] whose frequently published work, *A Serious Call to a Devout and Holy Life*, written in 1728, is well known. A new translation appeared in 1741.[74]

No one apparently contributed more to the spread of Brother Lawrence's influence in the English-speaking world than John Wesley, the founder of Methodism. Wesley read him to his faithful, even during his missionary journey in America in 1736.[75] After 1750 he republished Lawrence, among others, in his impressive collection, the "Christian Library."[76] He included Lawrence in the syllabus of his college in Kingswood and recommended him to all his disciples in the study plan for his associate preachers.[77]

Lawrence has been translated and retranslated, printed and reprinted by Anglicans, Protestants and Catholics in the United

Kingdom and especially in [North] America to the present day. In the eyes of many, Brother Lawrence ranks among the classics.[78] For example, Thomas Kelly, the outstanding Quaker, wrote: "With delight I read Brother Lawrence, in his *Practice of the Presence of God.*"[79]

Other Languages

Lawrence has been translated into other languages as well. There have already been, for example, five translations into Dutch (1842, 1910, 1954, 1956, 1976), and many reprints. In a recent study, Jure Zecevic states that Lawrence has been translated into English, German, Dutch, Spanish, Italian, Bengali, Hindi, Hebrew, Japanese, Swedish, and Croatian.[80] The list must be completed with Indonesian and Korean.[81]

Significance of Brother Lawrence's Writings

Our next consideration is Lawrence's contemporary relevance, not as a theoretician but as a truly practical counselor, a brother concerned about our well-being.

The Present Moment

God, the absolute mystery, the gentle one burning with love, invites us to approach him, the Presence *par excellence,* and experience him, even though we are restless, fascinated more by the superficial than by what is truly valuable. Before we can love, we are loved! A "great treasure" exists for the taking, but Lawrence warns that "we tie God's hands." This great living Reality would like to be the Source of life and meaning for us, but "we often block the flow of this torrent because of our lack of appreciation for it" (L 1). Let us open our eyes; all good will come to us at the same time! "The practice of the presence of God, in my opinion, is the essence of the spiritual life, and it seems to me that by practicing it properly, we become spiritual in no time.... If I were a preacher, I would preach nothing but the practice of the presence of God, and if I were a spiritual director, I would recommend it to everyone because I believe it is so necessary, and even easy" (L 3).

The Methodless Method

Indeed a beneficial practice! We must accept the dialogue God offers and enter into a relationship with him; otherwise the lover offers his gift in vain. But what is striking in the teaching of Lawrence, the nonintellectual opposed to elaborate methods,[82] is that he cracks the nutshell, frees the essential, goes directly toward the goal. This is what won him the esteem of so many people who, by way of life or circumstance, are "arhythmic," subject to the unforeseen, without schedule or regular pauses. Lawrence proposes a democratization and universalization of the search for God. He recommends a practice that must be maintained, like breathing, but "in holy liberty, without difficulty or anxiety" (L 4). "We do not always have to be in church to be with God," he wrote to a laywoman, advising her to turn occasionally to God present in her "heart" to "converse with him there" (L 9). "Do not burden yourself with rules or private devotions," he said to her, but "get used to gradually offering God your heart whenever you can" (note the skilled teacher's progression of thought). You need not flaunt this search for God, for "it cannot be detected by others" (L 6). In any event we must not say this practice is not for us. "Everyone is capable of these familiar conversations with God, some more than others; he knows what we can do" (L 9). The ex-soldier recommends his methodless method to a soldier (L 6). Lawrence never separates prayer from concrete life; rather he advocates their union.

Lawrence's credibility is enhanced because he knows what he is talking about when he speaks of the routine of daily life. He is "the mystic *par excellence* of the duties of one's state, of the humble life of tedious tasks."[83] He was a cook who knew stress, the pressure of busy times, the discontent of consumers, ingratitude, monotonous tasks, fatigue, disorder that must be straightened out, and the endless stack of dishes. Beginning with this foundation, and (it must be added) along with prolonged periods of nocturnal silence before God, he invites us to create for ourselves moments of interiority and Presence, to take advantage of the many "wasted" moments during the day, whether we live in an apartment on the Rue Vaugirard, or work in the kitchen of a restaurant now occupying the site of the former Carmelite monastery, or ride the metro that passes under the garden, or are teachers or students in the prestigious institutes that now take up Lawrence's house, or are seated before a computer in a Parisian office, or are behind the steering wheel driving down streets with countless red lights and a thousand faces, all children of God.

Pedagogue of Presence

Lawrence adapts his counsels to all circumstances, but the necessary prerequisite, before all else, is the desire "to learn the trade" (L 10). This "practice" will never become "second nature" (L 25) without "turning inward to God" (SM 9), without "often repeating these little adorations throughout the day" (L 6), without fostering this awareness (SM 29). Knowing how suspicious the believer is, how slow the disciple is, and how flighty our minds are (L 7), our realistic sandalmaker warned us that "the beginning is very difficult" (L 15); "in the beginning we often think the time spent is wasted" and we feel "repugnance" (L 4). We must commit ourselves decisively: "From this moment on we must make a firm resolution" (L 3), "be resolved to persevere until death, and in spite of all the difficulties" (L 4). "You will soon see the benefits!" "You will become spiritual in no time" (L 3). "Those who are empowered by the breath of the Holy Spirit sail along even when asleep" (L 1). Lawrence learned to "recall" his attention to God (L 4, 7). In the end, he experienced how God himself "recalled" his attention (L 1, 2). He summarized his approach: "This practice of the presence of God, somewhat difficult in the beginning, when practiced faithfully, secretly brings about marvelous effects in the soul, draws the abundance of God's grace upon it, and leads it imperceptibly to this simple awareness, to this loving view of God present everywhere, which is the holiest, the surest, the easiest, and the most efficacious form of prayer" (SM, 31). Everything becomes a "bridge" to approach God (CN 50).

We know the objection: This may be good for others but not for me, I'm too stuck to the ground. Christ, who came to save sinners (Mt 9:13), is our liberator. The request for liberation, the admission of our forgetfulness, the desire to return can effectively reopen the dialogue—if we have the old brother's humor. "When I realize I have failed, I admit it and say: this is typical, that's all I can do!" (CN 31). "I will never do anything right if you leave me alone; it's up to you to stop me from falling" (CN 16). If he had not preceded her by two centuries, one would think Lawrence's emphasis on merciful love and on the simplest things of each day (CN 19, 49) were borrowed from his little sister [St. Thérèse] of Lisieux.[84]

"I Dine at the Lord's Table"

Our cook said: "I can anticipate your reply, that I have it easy since I eat and drink at the Lord's table" (L 11). And it is undeniable. But his table is very large, and we are all invited to it. It is our responsibility to weigh our excuses (cf. Lk 14:15-24).

Lawrence of the Resurrection stands as a witness to the importance of the overwhelming, living experience of the presence of God. It is evident from his writings. But he is convinced the experience is not limited to himself alone. Listen to him carefully: "Sometimes the soul even becomes one continuous act because it constantly practices this divine presence. I know few persons reach this advanced state. It is a grace God bestows only on a few chosen souls, since this simple awareness remains ultimately a gift from his kind hand. But let me say, for the consolation of those who desire to embrace this holy practice, that he ordinarily gives it to souls who are disposed to it. If he does not give it, we can at least acquire, with the help of ordinary grace, a manner and state of prayer that greatly resembles this simple awareness by means of this practice of the presence of God" (SM 36-37). That *greatly resembles* this simple awareness....

Lawrence has not forgotten the long, difficult journey he made: "During this period, I fell often but I got back up just as quickly" (L 2). He realized no less the seriousness of God's demands: "The heart must be empty of everything else" (L 3). That is, the consuming fire of divine Mercy must bring about in us a "great purity of life" (SM 27). As a matter of fact, the practice of the presence of God sensitizes us to the Lord's will. Lawrence expresses it this way: "Not to do, say, or think anything that might displease him" (L 1, 2, 15). That is where this practice should lead! Jesus proclaimed its effect: "Blessed are the pure of heart, for they shall see God" (Mt 5:8).

There are in this world human beings in solitary places who have answered the Lord's call to make of their lives a little flame, always bright, always attentive to his Presence, in the heart of the Church. But there are others as well who are very active, in households and in the midst of men and women—these too are like little lights that illumine the city.

An Ecumenical Presence

Having indicated Brother Lawrence's interdenominational impact, we now quote the words of a Protestant brother to emphasize the extent of his ecumenical influence. "If we note the various editions of Brother Lawrence's works, we can see that he was able to speak to various Christian denominations. Because of his experience of the Presence of God, he belongs to a category beyond denominations, witnessing to a truth that is as proper to Protestantism as it is to Catholic Christianity, even though his Carmelite background cannot be denied. Though he lived in the seventeenth century when no one yet spoke of ecumenism, he was the herald of a Christianity that crossed all denominational lines." [85]

A Man Content

If we were to try to describe the effect of the practice of the presence of God on Brother Lawrence, we could use the same adjective he used two months before his death to summarize his good mood: "I am still very *content*. Everyone is suffering, and I, who should do rigorous penances, experience such continual, profound joys that I have trouble keeping them under control" (L 13). "I have been ready to die many times, although I had never been so *content* before" (L 15).

The etymology of the word indicates that contentment comes from the fact that everything "tends together" *[con-tendere]* toward its goal, that there is no internal division. Lawrence was a man of one purpose, straightforward, a rock, a stable, free being who found his simplicity, his harmony, and his dynamism in the presence of God, the source of his quiet glow. He breathed God because he breathed in God. "Having contemplated the eternal one for so long, he had become eternal like him," Beaufort said (W 17). He recognized everywhere the presence of God, whose love was already burning in the depths of his heart. Faith and experience united, enabling him to develop this unified vision in which everything became great, beautiful, fascinating, and unexpected, as a reflection and reminder of God. Even little things hide a secret, speak a message, and are the place of an encounter.

Ultimately the most profound significance of Lawrence's testimony is to show us how the practice of the presence of God can make the life of a little one—someone hidden, even insignificant—full, happy, and rich. A little bit of Nazareth in Paris! Just like the village carpenter and his wife who knew so well how to say "yes," and who could scarcely believe that God wanted to be so close to us, and forever.

NOTES

1. Pierre Pourrat, *Christian Spirituality* (Westminster, MD: Newman Press, 1955), vol. 4, *From Jansenism to Modern Times*, pp. 128-130.

2. Henri Bremond, *Histoire littéraire du sentiment religieux en France* (Paris: Bloud and Gay, 1923), vol. 6, *La Conquête mystique*, p. 392.

3. Titus Brandsma [beatified in 1985], "Carmes" in *Dictionnaire de spiritualité*, vol. 2, col. 162.

4. Aldous Huxley, *The Perennial Philosophy* (London: Chalto and Windus, 1947), p. 328.

5. Cf. Conrad De Meester, *Vie et Pensées du frère Laurent,* Foi vivante series (Paris: Editions du Cerf, "Foi vivante," 1991).

6. Cf. *Catalogus chronologicus et historicus carmelitarum discalceatorum provinciae parisiensis,* MS 1155, p. 218, Bibliotheque de l'Arsenal (Paris): "Brother Lawrence of the Resurrection, Nicolas, son of Dominique Herman and Louise Majeur, of the village of Hériminil (diocese of Toul), born in 1614, professed in Paris on 14 August 1642, died in Paris on 12 February 1691." See also *Necrologium carmelitarum discalceatorum provinciae parisiensis...a monastarium fundatione in Galliis ad annum 1718...* (Paris: J. B. Coignard, 1718), p. 86, no. 490: "Brother Lawrence of the Resurrection, lay brother, legal name Nicolas Herman, of Hériminil, diocese of Toul, born in 1614, professed 14 August 1642 in Paris, where he died on 12 February [1691, the year treated on this page of the *Necrologium*], at the age of 77, 49 years professed." The parish records of Hériménil from Lawrence's time no longer exist. Hériménil is located 4 kilometers from Lunéville and had a population of 751 in 1990.

7. The *Constitutions* of the Order (cf *Constitutiones fratrum discalceatorum congregationis S. Eliae ordinis beatissimae Virgini Mariae de Monte Carmelo* [Paris: Andre Chevalier, 1637] II, 4, 1) required the lay brothers to spend "two months in secular clothes" in the monastery before receiving the habit and beginning the novitiate, which lasted two years. We can determine the time of his entrance from the date of his profession.

8. The second [French] foundation (1611) of the reformed friars of St. Teresa of Avila. For information on the Paris monastery, see Appendix I.

9. Though not the custom in Carmel, examples do exist in which the patron saint of one's home parish became the inspiration of the religious's new name. The idea could have come from Lawrence himself.

10. At the time, the canonical novitiate for the province of Paris was located in Paris itself (see Appendix I).

11. Other examples can be given. Cf. L 4, L 12, and CN 17.

12. For a more detailed analysis see our *Vie et Pensées du frère Laurent*.

13. Louis de Sainte-Thérèse, *Annales des Carmes déchaussés de France de 1608 à 1665*, 2 vols., new ed., (Laval: Chailland, 1891), 2:831.

14. Louis de Sainte-Thérèse affirmed this for the years preceding 1649 (cf. *Annales*, 2:410). This number may have varied afterward (see Appendix I).

15. Another floor was added to the Paris monastery during the years 1674–1676. The presence of friars in formation, novices or scholastics, is evoked in EL 48.

16. Louis de Sainte-Thérèse often referred to the "collection" when he spoke of the lay brothers in the *Annales*. Lawrence would have done this less often as his physical problems increased, but his good judgment when seeking alms is nonetheless mentioned in W 3.

17. In the *Nouveau Supplément au grand dictionnaire historique, généalogique et géographique, etc. de M. Louis Moreri, pour servir à la dernière édition de 1732 et aux précédentes* (Paris: Jacques Vincent, 1749), 2:19: "From the time he entered the monastery, he reached such a high degree of perfection that all Paris admired him."

18. EL 39. This "outstanding bishop of France" could not have been Fénelon, as Suzanne Bucheraux assumed (cf. Laurent de la Résurrection, *L'Expérience de la présence de Dieu* [Paris: Editions du Seuil, 1948], pp. 58–59), since Lawrence died in 1691 and Fénelon did not become bishop until 1695, two years after these lines were written. A more likely candidate would be Msgr. Louis-Antoine de Noailles, future Cardinal Archbishop of Paris, for the simple reason that Lawrence's biographer was Noailles's confessor.

19. See text 38, Appendix III.

20. See text 27, Appendix III.

21. For example L 2, 3, 4, 12; EL 42–43; W 5.

22. See Teresa of Avila, *Foundations* 5, 8.

23. See SM 5, note 1; SM 18, notes 13 and 14; L 2, notes 4, 5, 6, 9, 11, and 12; L 5, note 3. Louis de Sainte-Thérèse reports the advice that Father Julien de la Croix gave to his Parisian novices, regarding the works of St. Teresa and St. John of the Cross, "alternately to read one for three months, and then the other, and then to begin again." See *Annales*, 2:898.

24. Louis de Sainte-Thérèse often emphasized the authority, in the Carmelite province of Paris, of the pedagogical works of John of Jesus and Mary, whether of the *Instruction of Novices* (Annales, I:80, 136, 164, 228; II:878, 894, 908), or of the *Disciplina Claustralis* (*Annales*, I:228). [For English translations of these works, see John of Jesus and Mary, *Instruction of Novices*, 2d ed. (New York: Benziger Brothers, 1930); and *Manual for Novices*, 2d ed. (New York: Benziger Brothers, 1921).] Regarding the influence of John of Jesus and Mary on Brother Lawrence see also EL 22, note 15; SM 9, note 3; SM 20, note 16; L 6, note 2.

25. Lawrence was not comfortable with rigid methods. See L 12, L 2; SM 6 and 7; CN 41 and 42.

26. Cf. *Constitutions*, I, 4, 4; and Louis de Sainte-Thérèse, *Annales*, I:101.

27. Their convent, on the Rue Cassette, adjoined the garden of the Discalced Carmelites; see Appendix I and note 2 of the Introductory Note to the *Letters*, p. 48.

28. On the question of the manuscript, see the Introductory Note to the *Maxims*, pp. 31–33 .

29. The conversations of 1666–1667. See the Introductory Note to the *Conversations*, pp. 87–88.

30. Some extracts are also found in SM; cf. pp. 105–106 .

31. He must have met with Brother Lawrence "often" (W 15). He also cites the testimony of an "outstanding French bishop" (EL 39), of Fénelon (W 16) and "other learned men, ecclesiastics and religious" (EL 39), various Carmelites (EL 30, 37, 39, 53, 54, 56, 58, 59) and one of his friends (EL 41 and 59).

32. Appendix II, pp. 141–149.

33. Since the question of "approbations" played a role in the Fénelon-Bossuet conflict, the actual text for the first volume is given here: "I have read the manuscript and these letters. Given at Paris, November 23, 1691. Courcier. Theologian of Paris." And: "Approbation given. Permission to publish, November 30, 1691. De la Reynie."

34. See Appendix III, pp. 155ff.

35. Louis Cognet, *Crépuscule des mystiques: Bossuet-Fénelon* (Tournai: Desclée and Co., 1858), p. 6.

36. Jacques Le Brun, "Quiétisme," in *Dictionnaire de spiritualité*, vol. 12, col. 2838.

37. "Les gazettes et les lardons de Hollande," quoted in his *Réponse de M. de Paris aux quatre lettres de M. de Cambrai* [Reply of the Archbishop of Paris to the four letters of the Archbishop of Cambrai] in *Oeuvres Complètes de Fénelon*, vol. 2 (Paris-Lille-Besançon,1848), p. 528.

38. This is what Marjorlaine Chevallier has stated, in "Bibliographie des ouvrages mystiques édités par Pierre Poiret," *Revue d'histoire de la spiritualité* 53 (1977): 329; and in his work, *Pierre Poiret, Bibliotheca dissidentium* 5 (Baden-Baden: Koerner, 1985), p. 184. Poiret wrote, in *De eruditione specialiora, tribus tractatibus...* (Amstelaedami: ex officina Wetsteniana, 1707), pp. 721–722, that apart from editing them, he had nothing to do with the first edition of these two books [of Madame Guyon], done in Belgium in 1699. See the following note for the interpretation of "Belgium."

39. The Latin term *Belgium* in the preceding note must be understood in a broad historical sense. In the same volume, in *Epistola de principiis et characteribus mysticorum,* p. 561, Pierre Poiret stated that the writings of "Brother Lawrence of the Resurrection...were reprinted in Holland, together with the opuscules of Madame Guyon in the edition of 1699."

40. Responsible for the publication of many of Poiret's works and those of his Protestant friends. Note that the fictitious name "De la Pierre" could evoke "Wetstein" [since both "pierre" and "stein" mean stone].

41. Pp. 334–335. He quotes himself, repeating *Epistola* (cf. note 39), p. 562.

42. See the Introductory Note to the *Practice,* note 1.

43. From the bibliography, p. 155, it is clear that "original" refers to the first *printed* edition.

44. This fourth edition, itself incomplete despite what the subtitle claims, mentions "a retranslation into French of an English translation" of Brother Lawrence published in Switzerland around 1894. For our purposes here, this French "retranslation" can be disregarded. Nevertheless, there have been several reprints: *La Présence de Dieu dans la vie de tous les jours: Lettres et entretiens par le Frère Laurent* [The Presence of God in Daily Life: Letters and Conversations of Brother Lawrence], 2d ed. (Geneva: Labor et Fides, n.d.). This contained the four conversations and fourteen of the sixteen letters. "The 'Conversations of Brother Lawrence' are like a spring of living water from which generations of souls have drunk avidly," writes Pierre Juillard in the Preface (p. 5). This text was "printed under the auspices of Les Veilleurs." Before this reprint edition (and even before our "fourth complete edition") this "retranslated" text had appeared in the form of a little brochure, *Entretiens et Lettres du frère Laurent sur la Présence de Dieu* (Le Veilleurs, n.d.), "Tiers-Ordre" ["Third Order"] protestant (sic). One printing was made at Alençon by A. Coueslant (44 pages); another in Lezay by A. Chopin (48 pages), for the librarie Fischbacher of Paris.

45. M. Van den Bossche used the first *printed* edition of 1692 for the text of the *Maxims,* and a "manuscript preserved in l'Arsenal" (MS 2362) for the *Ways and Conversations* (cf. pp. 15–16). But in fact the latter is only a transcription of the printed edition of 1694, which includes the approbation of de Noailles, as Suzanne Boucheraux has already noted (cf. *L'Expérience de la présence de Dieu,* p. 34).

46. François de Sainte-Marie, "L'esprit de la Règle du Carmel," *Ephemerides Carmeliticae* 2 (1948): 223.

47. This is also the case for the preceding edition, edited by Suzanne Boucheraux, whose abilities as a historian and researcher are evident in her thesis on *La Réforme des Carmes en France et Jean de Saint-Samson* [Reform of the Carmelites in France and John of St. Sampson], (Paris: Vrin, 1950).

48. Though in this matter one should never lose hope. Regarding MS 6129 of the Bibliotheque de l'Arsenal, a folio describing 250 manuscripts located at the Carmelite library, Rue Vaugirard, at the time of its confiscation in 1791 (p. 23), mentions two copies of the *"Spiritual Maxims of 1692"* (this must involve a *manuscript* copy of the book *printed* in 1692 after Lawrence's death) and two copies of the *Life and Ways of Brother Lawrence* (also a copy, see note 45). Pisani indicates that "this library was dispersed during the Revolution" (see Appendix I). A certain number of these manuscripts have been preserved by the bibliothèque de l'Arsenal, but there is no further mention of Brother Lawrence.

49. "Avis de l'imprimeur" in *La Théologie de la présence de Dieu...*, p. 2.

50. See text 5 of Appendix III. The following text indicates that Bossuet already knew the contents of the *Letter* a month before its appearance, suggesting that he collaborated on it. See note to Appendix II, pp. 137ff.

51. See text 6 of Appendix III.

52. See text 17 of Appendix III.

53. The Chancery of Châlons-sur-Marne where Beaufort was vicar general. During those years a real friendship existed between de Noailles and Fénelon, who was greatly respected by Bossuet.

54. This is what Abbé de Beaumont tells us in a letter of 1732. See *Oeuvres complètes de Fénelon*, vol. 10 (Paris-Lille-Besançon, 1852), p. 57. In Appendix III we will see that Fénelon knew Beaufort well in Paris; see text 20.

55. Fénelon especially interested in the *Ways,* since Msgr. de Noailles had approved and recommended them (cf. Henri Sanson, *St. Jean de la Croix entre Bossuet et Fénelon: Contribution à l'étude de la querelle du Pur Amour* [Paris: PUF, 1953], p. 50). Fénelon must have been familiar with the first volume of Brother Lawrence, that of the *Maxims,* for Beaufort spoke of it openly in the *Ways* (W 1). His copy of the book of the *Maxims* may have been lost in a fire that destroyed Fénelon's episcopal residence, "with all its furniture, books, and papers." When Fénelon, who was away, learned the news [of the fire], he said, "Better my house than the cottage of some poor laborer." See "Histoire de Fénelon" in *Oeuvres complètes*, vol. 10, p. 89.

56. For example, Jacques Le Brun in Fénelon, *Oeuvres,* "Bibliotheque de la Pléiade" series (Paris: Gallimard, 1983), 1:1612; Jean Orcibal (with the collaboration of Jacques Le Brun and Irénée Noye), in *Correspondance de Fénelon* (Genève-Paris: Droz, 1987), 7:98; Jean Orcibal, "Les spirituels français et espagnols chez John Wesley et ses contemporains," *Revue de l'histoire des religions* 139 (1951): 108; Levesque and Urbain in *Correspondance de Bossuet* (Paris: Hachette), 8: 386.

57. See *Manuscrit Dom Jalloutz* (Archives de l'abbaye de Sept-Fons), p. 591 and F[rère] B[enoît], *Étude historique sur l'abbaye de Notre Dame de St. Lieu Sept Fons depuis sa fondation jusqu'à ce jour* (n.p., 1873), pp. 61–70 and 95–96 for information common to Joseph and Eustache de Beaufort.

58. According to Document G 32, in the G series (secular clergy), in the departmental archives of Marne.

59. According to Jean Orcibal (*Correspondance de Fénelon* [Paris: Klincksieck, 1976], 5:116), Joseph de Beaufort was "the son of a rich merchant of Rue St. Denis"; he was named chaplain to the Incurables on 1 February 1669, and died "in 1711." Among other works on the spiritual life, he had published the *Traité de l'origine et de la perfection de la religion chrétienne*, which was often attributed to de Noailles himself; see the article "Noailles" in *Dictionnaire de théologie catholique*, vol. XI, col. 678.

60. Fénelon often recalled these facts. See, e.g., text 20 in Appendix III.

61. This is the translation of the second edition of Brother Lawrence in *Recueil de divers traités...: Etliche vortreffliche tratätlein aus der geheimen Gottes-Gelehrtheit...heraus gegeben von G.A.* (Frankfurt and Leipzig: Joh. Konig, 1701).

62. The information presented in *L'Expérience*, p. 34 is not entirely accurate, as when Suzanne Boucheraux writes that "the German-speaking countries had a translation thanks to Clemens Auguste von Droste zu Vischering, the future archbishop of Cologne, ...in 1829."

63. See Max Wieser, *Peter Poiret: Der vater der romanischer Mystik in Deutschland* (Munich: Müller, 1932), pp. 106–107; see also Gerhard Tersteegen, in the work mentioned in note 69 below, p.167.

64. *Theologie von der Gegenwart Gottes...ins Teutsche versetz durch Joh. Mich. Schoppach* (Frankfurt: Seidel, 1714).

65. Gottfried Arnold, *Das Leben der Glaubigen...in Zusass einiger besondern Zeugnisse der Wahrheit und Lebensbeschreibungen...* (Halle: Wäysenhaus, 1701), appendix to vol. 4, pp. 169–192.

66. Johann Heinrich Reitz, *Historie der Wiedergeborenen* (Idstein: Verlag Haug, 1717), 3:106ff.

67. Walter Nigg, *Grosse Heiligen* (Zurich and Munich: Artemis, 1981), pp. 396–397. On Tersteegen, see the articles (with bibliographies) of Gerhard Ruhbach, "Gerhard Tersteegen," in *Grosser Mystiker: Leben und Wirken*, ed. Gerhard Ruhbach and Josef Sudbrack (Munich: Beck, 1984), pp. 252–266, 386–389; and Bernd Jaspert, "Tersteegen," in *Dictionnaire de spiritualité*, vol. XV, col. 260–271.

68. Winifried Zeller, "Die kirchengeschichtliche Sicht des Mönchtums im Protestantismus, insbesonders bei Gerhard Tersteegen," in *Erbe und Auftrag* 49 (1973): 23.

69. Gerhard Tersteegen, *Auserlesene Lebensbeschreibungen heiliger Seelen* (Essen: Verlag Z. Badeker, 1784–1786), 2:168. On the presence of Brother Lawrence in the spirituality of Tersteegen, see especially Giovanna della Croce, "Gerhard Tersteegen e il Carmelo," in *Ephemerides Carmeliticae* 24

(1973): 375–401; Walter Nigg, "Bruder Lorenz," in *Der verborgene Glanz oder die paradoxale Lobpreisung* (Olten and Fribourg-en-Brisgau: Walter-Verlag, 1974), pp. 109–146; Margarete Fritzsche, "Bruder Laurentius und Gerhard Tersteegen," in *Weg zum wahren Glauben* (Gütersloh: Gütersloher Verlagshaus Gerd Mohn, 1980), pp. 33–48.

70. Jean Orcibal, "L'influence spirituelle de Fénelon dans les pays anglo-saxons au XVIIIe siecle," *XVIIe siècle: Bulletin de la Société d'étude du XVIIe siècle* 12–14 (1951–1952): 278.

71. *Ibid.*, p. 286.

72. Cf. Jean Orcibal, "Les spirituels français et espagnols chez John Wesley et ses contemporains," *Revue de l'histoire des religions* 139 (1951): 63; and "L'originalité theologique de John Wesley et les spiritualités du Continent," *Revue historique* 222 (1959): 54. This translation of Brother Lawrence contained some of Fénelon's thoughts and was called *Devotional Tracts concerning the Presence of God and other Religious Subjects.*

73. Cf. Orcibal, *ibid.*

74. Cf. Orcibal, "Les spirituels," p. 95, note 171. The title of this translation was *The Great Advantages that arise to a Christian by preserving in his Mind a Constant Sense of the Divine Presence: Set forth in the life of Nicolas Herman* (Edinburgh, 1641).

75. Cf. Orcibal, "Les spirituels," p. 63.

76. Cf. Orcibal, "Les spirituels," p. 62; and "L'originalité," p. 61.

77. Cf. Orcibal, "Les spirituels," p. 180; and "L'originalité," pp. 61–62.

78. Cf. AA.VV., *An Introduction to Five Spiritual Classics* (New York: Christian Service Board of the Methodist Church, 1955), pp. 75–104 [by Lillian W. Pope]. The other four classics were St. Augustine, Thomas à Kempis, William Law and Thomas Kelly; Richard Foster, *The Celebration of Discipline* (New York: Harper & Row, 1978), chaps. 2 and 5; and Thomas Kelly, *A Testament of Devotion* (London: Quaker Home Service, 1979), p. 79, where Brother Lawrence is compared with St. Augustine's *Confessions* and the *Imitation of Christ.*

79. Thomas Kelly, *A Testament of Devotion*, p. 111. See also Frank Laubach's fervent praise of Brother Lawrence in *An Introduction to Five Spiritual Classics*, p. 76, as proof of the high regard for Brother Lawrence in many Protestant circles.

80. Jure Zecevic, "Nicolas Herman: Leben und Werk," *Teresianum* 35 (1984): 243. He may have consulted the International Carmelite Library of the Teresianum in Rome.

81. Thanks to the annual bibliographies of *Carmelus* (since 1953), *Archivum Bibliographicum Carmelitanum* (since 1955), and *Bibliographia Internationalis Spiritualitatis* (since 1966), we can now track publications concerning Brother Lawrence.

82. See note 25.

83. François de Sainte-Marie, Préface in *L'Experience*, p. 13.

84. The influence could have been the opposite, just as the emphasis on the "depths and center of the soul" would have appealed to Elizabeth of the Trinity (Dijon, 1880–1906). But neither of the libraries of the Carmels of Lisieux or Dijon contained any of Lawrence's writings. We have no intermediary source other than Ferdinand de Sainte-Thérèse, *Ménologe du Carmel: Vie des saints, bienheureux, vénérables, serviteurs de Dieu et personnages illlustres par leur piété de l'Ordre de N.-D. du Mont-Carmel...*, (Lille-Bruges: Desclée de Brouwer, 1879), which devotes only twelve lines to Lawrence, on p. 138.

85. Walter Nigg, *Der verborgene Glanz*, p. 141.

I

EULOGY

8

L'Eglise des CARMES DESCHAVSSÉS, *au bout du Fauxbourg* St *Germain, du costé du Parc, du Palais d'Orleans a Paris.*
chez P. *Mariette.*

Dessigné et gravé par L. *Maret.*
Auec prauilege du Roy

Seventeenth-century engraving, by Jean Marot, of the church of Discalced Carmelite friars in Paris as Brother Lawrence knew it. The monastery to the left, however, was greatly enlarged during Lawrence's time; see Appendix 1. (With permission of the Bibliothèque Nationale of Paris.)

Introductory Note
to the Eulogy

It was Joseph de Beaufort, a priest from Paris, though at the time vicar general of the bishop of Châlons-sur-Marne, who composed this "Testimony for Brother Lawrence of the Resurrection" published in 1692, a year after his death.

The reader will immediately note the rather panegyric style in which the ecclesiastic expressed his profound veneration for his humble Parisian friend. We can adjust to it quickly, yet without losing the impression that the events appear somewhat dramatized and the formulations fairly stereotyped. Nicolas Herman's parents "only taught him holy maxims in keeping with the Gospels" (EL 7). "After harsh inner struggles, after tears and sighs" (EL 11), Nicolas decided to become a religious and overcame "all the difficulties that the world and the devil ordinarily present to those who seek to change their lives" (EL 12). In the monastery, "their concern about his worth, and the esteem that he had acquired by heroic acts of virtue, made the novice master increase the difficulties to test his vocation and the determination of his spirit" (EL 20). During his great inner trial Brother Lawrence was often "completely bathed in tears" (EL 22), until in his "extreme misery" (EL 25) he "saw a ray of divine light" (EL 27); soon the "powers of hell that never tire of fighting against us no longer dared attack Lawrence" (EL 34).

But it would be unfair to list only the exaggerated and baroque expressions that Beaufort, a child of his times, used to sketch his friend's journey. We should rather appreciate how he rightly condenses Brother Lawrence's spiritual life around the three theological virtues of faith, hope and love (EL 42–50 & 56–58) without attributing to his mystic friend the extraordinary phenomena that the medieval hagiographers would often use to embellish their heros.

3

Once we have gotten into Beaufort's style we can grasp the essence of what he, very honestly, wanted to communicate.

Needless to say, we prefer the writings of Brother Lawrence himself over the words of the hagiographer. Lawrence's speech is simpler, more direct, his *own*. When we read both Lawrence's *Letters* and Beaufort's summary of them we can clearly see the differences of style.[1]

Finally, we point out that the original title, "Eulogy for Brother Lawrence of the Resurrection," is preceded by a "note to the reader" in the first edition (here EL 1–5), which served as an introduction to the complete volume of the *Maxims*. Here we have combined the two texts, which fit together perfectly. For, as we will see, Joseph de Beaufort is a very intelligent man, and the logic of his writing is impeccable.

NOTE

1. By using quotation marks in EL 28, Beaufort gives the impression of quoting Lawrence's own words as taken from his letters. This is nothing but an illusion. The terms "phantoms," "dreams," "languor," "dazzled," and "dissipate" do not appear in Lawrence's writings.

Eulogy

NOTE TO THE READER

1. Although this past year death has taken from us several Discalced Carmelites, priests and lay brothers, who in dying have left rare examples of all the religious virtues, it seems that Providence wanted us to take more particular note of Brother Lawrence of the Resurrection than of the others.

2. Here is the way Providence made known the merit of this saintly religious, who throughout his life deliberately hid himself from the view of others, and whose sanctity was not recognized until his death. Several pious people, having seen a copy of one of his letters, wanted to see more of them. It is for this reason that we have taken the trouble to collect what we could find of those he himself had written. Among them we found a manuscript entitled *Spiritual Maxims or the Means to Acquire the Presence of God*.

3. These maxims and letters are so edifying, so full of fervor, and are considered to be of such good style by those who had the comfort of reading them, that they did not want to be the only ones who benefited from them. They wanted the maxims and letters to be published, judging rightly that they would be most useful to souls seeking perfection by the practice of the presence of God.

4. And because there is nothing more eloquent than good example, we thought that, to make the work more complete, it was appropriate to include in the beginning a brief sketch of the author's life, where you will see such a true correspondence between his words and deeds that it will be evident he spoke only from his own experience.

5. All Christians will find matter for edification here. Those involved in the world will see how mistaken they are in seeking peace

and happiness in the empty glamour of passing things. Good people will find material to encourage them to persevere in the practice of virtue. Religious people, especially those who are not engaged in the salvation of souls [through active ministry], will be able to profit more than others, since they will be able to identify with one of their brothers. He, like them, had many duties to perform and yet, in the midst of the most demanding occupations, knew how to integrate action with contemplation so well that for more than forty years he almost never turned away from the presence of God, as you will see in some detail from what follows.

In Praise of Brother Lawrence of the Resurrection

6. It is an unchanging truth of Scripture that God's arm is not short,[1] and his mercy can never be exhausted by our sins. The power of his grace is no less great today than when the Church first came into existence. Since God wanted a continuous line of saints who would offer him worship worthy of his grandeur and majesty until the end of the world, and who, by the sanctity of their example, would be models of virtue, he was not satisfied merely to bring forth extraordinary men and women in the first centuries who worthily carried out this double obligation. God still raises up from time to time those who perfectly fulfill these two duties and who, preserving within themselves the first fruits of the Spirit, transmit them and make them come alive in others.

7. The one I am praising is Brother Lawrence of the Resurrection, a Discalced Carmelite friar whom God recently raised up to offer him due homage and to encourage the friars in the practice of all the virtues by the rare example of his piety. His name in the world was Nicolas Herman.[2] His mother and father were fine people who led an exemplary life. They inspired the fear of God in him from his childhood and took particular care for his education, presenting him only with holy maxims in keeping with the Gospel.

8. He was born in Hériménil in Lorraine,[3] a province whose conflicts would affect him. He went into the army[4] where, walking in simplicity and righteousness, God preserved him by his goodness and mercy. He was taken prisoner by German troops[5] on the march and was treated as a spy. The extent of his patience and tranquility

under these terrible circumstances cannot be imagined. They even threatened to hang him. He fearlessly answered that he was not what they suspected. He viewed death with indifference, because his conscience reproached him for no crime. When the soldiers saw his courage they released him.

9. The Swedes entered Lorraine, and while passing through the area attacked the little town of Rambervillers [6] where our young soldier was wounded, thus forcing him to withdraw to the nearby home of his parents.[7]

10. As a result of this incident he left the military to undertake a holier profession and fight under the standard of Jesus Christ. It was not vain transports of indiscreet zeal that turned him away from so tumultuous a state; rather, sentiments of true piety led him to resolve to give himself completely to God and to rectify his past conduct. This God of all consolation[8] who destined him for a holier life let him glimpse the emptiness of the world's vanities, and touched him with the love of celestial things.

11. These initial impulses of grace, however, did not entirely achieve their effect. He often relived the perils of his military service, the vanity and corruption of the times, the instability of other people, the treason of an enemy, and the infidelity of his friends. It was only after intense reflection, inner struggles, sighs, and tears that, overcome by the power of eternal truths, he firmly resolved to devote himself to the practice of the Gospel and to follow in the footsteps of his uncle,[9] a holy Discalced Carmelite who helped him see that the air of the world is contagious, and that if it doesn't kill those who breathe it, at the very least it impairs them and corrupts those who follow its ways.

12. The wise counsel of this enlightened director [10] opened the way of perfection to Herman, and the fine dispositions of his own soul likewise contributed greatly. His good sense, his prudence, evident on his face, soon lifted all the obstacles that the world and the devil ordinarily place before those who desire to change their lives. The prudent assurance, natural to him, that motivated him so completely, lifted him up miraculously and in a moment's time. He was changed into a new man by meditating on his baptismal promises, on the disorder of his youth, on the mysteries of our Christian faith, and especially on the Passion of Jesus Christ, which he could

never think about without being deeply moved, for the humility of the cross seemed more beautiful to him than all the glory of the world.

13. Thus inflamed with divine fervor he sought God, according to the apostle's counsel, in simplicity and sincerity of heart.[11] His only thoughts were for solitude so he could weep for his sins. Given his mature age, he could no longer be accused of being impetuous, and so he seriously considered withdrawing from the world. The opportunity for it appeared favorable to him, as I will explain.

14. A gentleman, well off by this world's standards but nonetheless dissatisfied with himself and always uneasy in the midst of his wealth, became convinced that God alone could satisfy the depths of his desires. Because he preferred evangelical poverty to all the world's treasures, he ran off to a hermitage to taste how sweet the Lord is to those who seek him in truth. Our Herman likewise took advantage of so blessed an opportunity. His soul, now tired of the unhappy life he was leading, began to desire rest. Accompanied by such a faithful guide, nothing hindered him from withdrawing to the desert, where the Christian zeal that motivated him dissipated his fears, and he was able to cling to God more than ever.

15. Although the eremitical life is excellent for the advanced and the perfect, it is not ordinarily the best way for beginners. Our new solitary realized this clearly as he saw joy, sadness, peace, disturbance, fervor, distraction, trust and despondency reign one after the other in his heart, and he therefore began to doubt the validity of his way. He decided to enter a community to embrace a way of life whose rule—founded as it was, not on the shifting sands of passing devotion, but on the sturdy rock of Jesus Christ, the foundation of all religious life—would strengthen him against the instability of his conduct.

16. Frightened nonetheless by the prospect of a perpetual struggle, and perhaps tempted by the devil, he could not commit himself. Each day he was less resolved, until once again he listened to the voice of God who called him with such tenderness. He went to Paris where he asked for the religious habit and was received among the brothers of the Order of Discalced Carmelites. He was given the name Brother Lawrence of the Resurrection.[12]

17. From the beginning of his novitiate he applied himself to the exercises of religious life with great fervor. He had singular affection for the Blessed Virgin Mary and was especially devoted to her. He had a filial trust in her protection. She was his refuge in all the problems of his life, in the troubles and anxieties that disturbed his soul, and therefore he would call her "his good mother."

18. In particular, he devoted himself to the practice of mental prayer. No matter how great his occupations were, they were never an excuse for missing this holy exercise. The presence of God, and the love it produced, were his favorite virtues, and they made him a model for his fellow novices in a short time. The victorious grace of Jesus Christ made him ardently embrace penance and look for the austerities that nature flees with such aversion.

19. Although his superiors assigned him to the most menial duties, Lawrence never uttered a complaint. On the contrary, grace sustained him in those unpleasant and boring tasks, never discouraged by what is bitter and harsh. He willingly accepted whatever natural repugnance he felt, considering himself fortunate to suffer or to be humiliated after the example of the Savior.[13]

20. His acts of virtue won him the esteem of all. The novice master, however, concerned for his well-being, found it necessary to increase the difficulties, in order to test his vocation and the strength of his spirit. He assigned him various tasks to strengthen his soul. This testing did not discourage him; rather, he bore it with all the fidelity you might expect. This was proven again on another occasion when a friar came to him saying that they were talking about dismissing him from the monastery. This was his reply: "I am in the hands of God, and he can do with me as he pleases. I do not act out of human respect, and if I cannot serve God here, I will do so elsewhere."

21. When the time came for his profession,[14] he offered himself completely to God without hesitation or reservation. I could cite here several noble acts that deserve special attention and would convince the reader of the fullness of his sacrifice, but I will pass over them in silence in order to elaborate more on the inner struggles that afflicted his soul, partly by order of divine Providence, which permitted them to purify him, and partly due to his lack of experience, for he wanted to walk in the spiritual life according to his own

manner. He saw the sins of his past life, and this sight horrified him and made him appear so little and so wretched in his own eyes that he judged himself unworthy of the least caresses of the Bridegroom. Nonetheless, he also saw himself extraordinarily favored, and in the humble estimation he had of his own lowliness he did not dare accept the heavenly blessings God was giving him. He did not yet know that God was merciful enough to communicate himself to a sinner, such as Lawrence considered himself to be.

22. The fear of self-deception began to take strong hold of his heart, and his state appeared so uncertain that he no longer knew what would become of him. This consequently caused him such terrible torments that he could only convey them by comparing them to those of hell. In this deplorable state, he often went to a private place near his pantry where there was a picture of Christ bound to the pillar.[15] There, his heart distraught, and completely bathed in his tears, he poured out his feelings before his God and begged him not to let him perish, because he had placed all his trust in him and intended only to please him.

23. No matter how he prayed, however, fears and disturbing anxieties increased his pain so that, all at once, his spirit was paralyzed. The solitude he had regarded as a safe haven now seemed like a stormy sea. His spirit was disturbed like a ship beaten by winds and storm, abandoned by its captain, and he did not know what to do nor how to resolve this, for, on the one hand, he experienced a secret inclination to surrender to the Lord by a continual immolation of himself; and on the other, the fear that he had strayed from the ordinary path [to holiness] led him to innocently resist God. All these prospects, so deplorable to nature, filled him with terror and dread. Furthermore, he received no help from heaven or earth, so his soul was plunged into bitterness and thick darkness.

24. This experience, difficult as it may be, is nonetheless what God often uses to test the virtue of his true servants before giving them the inestimable treasure of his wisdom. This is what he did with Brother Lawrence. The extent of his patience, his moderation, his resolution and his tranquility in the midst of these trials cannot be imagined. He truly expected only suffering and humiliation because he was humble in his thoughts and actions. Therefore he asked only for the chalice of the Lord, and he drank all the bitterness from it.

25. If only it had pleased God to grant him a bit of the consolation he had felt at the beginning of his penance! But no, everything was taken from him! Ten years of fear and suffering left him with very little relief. He had no taste for prayer and could find no alleviation of his sufferings. That is what made his life so difficult and reduced him to such misery that his life became unbearable, and his only support was faith.

26. In this sea of different thoughts where he was reduced to extremes, his courage remained steadfast. In fact, even in the midst of his greatest sufferings, he always had recourse to prayer, to the practice of the presence of God, to the practice of all the Christian and religious virtues, to physical austerities, to sighs and tears, to long vigils, sometimes spending almost entire nights before the Blessed Sacrament.[16] When at last one day, he was reflecting on the sufferings that afflicted his soul, and knowing that it was for the love of God and for fear of displeasing him that he was enduring them, he made a firm resolution to bear them, not only for the rest of his life, but even for all eternity if it pleased God to so ordain it. "It doesn't matter what I do or what I suffer so long as I remain lovingly united to his will in all things," he said.

27. This was exactly the disposition God wanted him to have so he could fill him with his graces, and the resolve of his heart increased more than ever from that very moment. And God who needs neither time nor much reasoning to make himself understood, opened his eyes all at once. Lawrence saw a ray of divine light that illumined his mind, dissipated his fears, and put an end to his suffering. The graces he received more than compensated for all the afflictions of the past.

28. He thus experienced what St. Gregory described, namely, that the world seems very insignificant to a soul that contemplates the grandeurs of God.[17] His letters written to a Carmelite nun bear this out, and here in a few words is what they contain.[18]

> The entire world seems incapable of keeping me company. All that I see with the eyes of my body passes before me like phantoms and dreams, whereas all that I see with the eyes of my soul is my only desire. That I still find myself somewhat distant from the vision of God is the reason for my anguish and torment. Overwhelmed, on one hand, by the brightness of this divine

Sun of Justice who dissipates the shadows of the night, and paralyzed, on the other hand, because of my wretchedness, I am
often beside myself. Nonetheless, my most ordinary occupation
is to remain in the presence of God with all the humility of a
useless yet faithful servant.

29. This holy exercise shaped his special character, and the
habit he had formed became so natural to him that, as he explained
in one of his letters and in his other writings,[19] he spent the last forty
years of his life in an actual exercise of the presence of God, or
rather, as he himself said,[20] in a silent, intimate conversation with
him.

30. One day a friar, to whom Lawrence was obliged to reply,
asked him what means he had used to acquire the habit of the presence of God, the practice of which was so easy, so continual to him.
He answered:

From the moment I entered religious life, I considered God to
be the goal and end of all my soul's thoughts and affections. At
the beginning of my novitiate, during the hours consecrated to
mental prayer, I spent my time learning to appreciate the truth
of this divine Being, more so by the light of faith than by the
work of meditation and discourse. By this short and sure means,
I advanced in the knowledge of this amiable object with whom
I resolved to remain forever. Therefore, completely penetrated
by the grandeur of the infinite Being, I would enclose myself in
the place obedience had marked out for me, the kitchen.
There, alone, once my duties were taken care of, I devoted what
time remained to mental prayer, before as well as after my work.
When I began my work I said to God with filial trust: "My God,
since you are with me, and since I must apply myself to these
duties by your order, I beg you to give me the grace to remain
with you and keep you company. Even better, my Lord, work
with me, accept my efforts and take possession of all my affections." Thus during my work I continued to speak intimately
with him, offering him my little services, asking him for his
graces. When my work was completed, I examined the manner
in which I had done it and if I found any good in it, I thanked
God. But if I noticed any mistakes, I asked pardon and, without
getting discouraged, I redirected my mind and began again to

abide with God as if I had never moved away from him. Thus, by getting back up after my falls, and by the multiplicity of acts of faith and love, I arrived at a state in which it would have been just as impossible not to think about God as it was difficult to get used to doing so in the beginning.

31. Since he experienced the great benefits this holy exercise brings to the soul, he advised all his friends to apply themselves to it with all the care and fidelity possible. In order to encourage them to undertake it with firm resolution and invincible courage, he gave them such strong, convincing reasons that he not only influenced their minds but even penetrated their hearts. He made them love and undertake this holy practice with a degree of fervor equal to the indifference with which they had formerly regarded it. He had the gift to persuade those who approached him not only by his words, but also by his good example. You only had to look at him to be edified and put yourself in the presence of God, no matter how preoccupied you might be.

32. He maintained that the practice of the presence of God was the shortest, easiest way to arrive at Christian perfection, the form and life of virtue, and the great protection from sin. He insisted that this practice required only courage, good will, and the truth of deeds rather than words. It was evident from his conduct that when he carried out his duties as cook—even in the midst of his work, including the most distracting tasks—his mind was recollected in God. Although his tasks were great and difficult, often doing by himself what would require two, you never saw him act hurriedly, but always with appropriate moderation. He gave each task the time called for, always keeping his modest, tranquil air, working neither too fast nor too slow, remaining in the same evenness of spirit and constant peace.[21]

33. He carried out this office with all the love possible during a period of about thirty years,[22] until Providence ordained otherwise. His leg became ulcerated, so his superiors had to assign him to an easier task.[23] This change afforded him more leisure to adore God in spirit and in truth according to his inclination, allowing him to foster a more perfect awareness of God's presence by this exercise of faith and love.

34. In this intimate union brought about exclusively by these two virtues [i.e., faith and love], the images of creatures, effaced only with difficulty, were erased from his imagination. The powers of hell that never give up the fight against us no longer dared attack Lawrence. His passions became so peaceful that he was hardly aware of them any more. If they occasionally aroused some little emotion to humble him, he resembled those high mountains safe from nature's storms at their base.

35. From that time on he seemed to be naturally disposed to virtue, gentle in mood, completely righteous, with the best heart in the world. His fine countenance, his human, affable air, his simple, modest manner won him the esteem and good will of all who saw him. The more closely you looked, the more you discovered in him a depth of integrity and piety rarely found elsewhere. People noticed that one of his concerns was not to let any singularity show in his actions. He always followed the simplicity of the common life without putting on the austere, melancholy air that only serves to discourage people. He was not one of those inflexible people who consider sanctity incompatible with ordinary manners. He associated with everyone and never put on airs, acting kindly toward his brothers and friends without wanting to be conspicuous.

36. Far from boasting of God's graces and attempting to make his virtues show to attract esteem, he consistently applied himself to leading a hidden, unknown life. Just as the proud seek every means imaginable to obtain for themselves an advantageous place in the eyes of others, you could say that one who is truly humble makes every effort, not only to avoid the applause and praise of creatures, but even to withdraw from the honorable estimations creatures could have of him. We have come across saints in former ages who deliberately did ridiculous things to attract everyone's contempt and mockery, or at least to inspire doubts regarding the high opinions conceived of their worth. That is what Brother Lawrence did. His humility, which I consider his special trait, led him to use holy deceptions and some apparently childish behavior to conceal his virtue and hide its brightness.[24] He was looking for truth, not glory. And since he wanted God to be the sole witness of his actions, he wanted God alone for his reward.

37. Reserved as Lawrence was when it came to himself, he was, nonetheless, willing to speak for the sake of the edification of his brothers, not with the most enlightened whose knowledge and insights often inflate their hearts, but with the little and simplest ones; and it was noted that when he found those of this bent he hid nothing from them. He taught them the marvelous secrets of the interior life and the treasures of divine wisdom with admirable simplicity. The fervor that accompanied his words so enchanted those who had the advantage of conversing with him that they went off entirely penetrated with love for God, and completely inflamed with the desire to put into practice the great truths he had just taught them in secret.

38. Since God was leading him more by love than by fear of his judgments, so too all his spiritual conversations [25] were aimed at inspiring this same love, breaking the least attachments to creatures, and putting to death the old man to establish the reign of the new man.[26] "If you want to make great progress in the spiritual life," he would say to his brothers, "pay no attention to the beautiful words or the subtle discourse of the wise of the earth. Woe to those who look to human knowledge to satisfy their curiosity. It is the Creator who teaches the truth, who instructs the hearts of the humble in a moment,[27] and who makes them understand more regarding the mysteries of our faith and of the Divinity itself than if they had meditated on these things for many years."

39. It was for this reason that he carefully avoided answering questions of idle curiosity, which lead nowhere and only serve to encumber the mind and dry up the heart. But when his superiors ordered him to openly state his thoughts on the questions raised during his conversations, he answered so correctly and so clearly that no one could take exception to his replies. Several experts, ecclesiastic and religious, noticed this when they obliged him to answer them. This was also the wise opinion of an outstanding bishop of France,[28] whose conversations with Brother Lawrence led him to speak in his favor, saying that Lawrence had become worthy of God, who truly communicated with him, and who revealed to him his mysteries. He added that the grandeur and purity of Lawrence's love for God made him live in anticipation here on earth like the blessed in heaven.

40. He was raised up to God by the knowledge of creatures, convinced that the books of the greatest schools teach little compared with the great book of the world, when studied properly. His soul, touched by the diversity of the many elements that compose the world, was brought to God so forcefully that nothing could separate him from God. He noticed in each of its marvels the various attributes of the power, the wisdom, and the goodness of the Creator, who delighted his spirit in admiration and lifted up his heart in transports of love and joy, making him cry out with the Prophet: "O Lord, God of gods, how incomprehensible you are in your thoughts, how deep in your designs, and how powerful in all your actions!"[29]

41. He wrote such lofty and tender things on the grandeurs of God and on the ineffable communications of his love to souls that those who saw some of the sheets taken from his writings—which he loaned out only reluctantly and on condition that they be returned right away—were so enchanted and edified by them that they could only speak of them with admiration. In spite of his concern to hide them, we were nonetheless able to collect a few fragments. If only we were able to find the others! For, judging from what we can gather from the letters available to us and from his maxims, we have every reason to believe, as he himself declared to one of his friends, that these little works are nothing other than the outpourings of the Holy Spirit and the product of his love. He sometimes expressed these sentiments on paper, but on comparing what he had just written with what he experienced within, he considered his writings so inferior and so removed from his exalted awareness of God's grandeur and goodness that he often felt obliged to tear them up right then and there. He tore them up as willingly as he had written them because he had done so only to relieve his fullness, to let his spirit soar, to expand his heart and breast, too narrow to contain the divine fire that consumed him and made him suffer so strangely. His experience was comparable to a basin that overflows, unable to contain its waters, or else to an underground cavern that, unable to curtail the vehemence of the fire it encloses, is forced to release it.

42. Faith was the principal virtue among all those Brother Lawrence possessed.[30] The just live by this theological virtue, and thus it was the life and nourishment of his spirit. It fostered such

growth in his soul that you could see he made great progress in the spiritual life. It was this beautiful virtue that put the whole world under his feet and made him so lowly in his own eyes that in his heart he considered himself unworthy of taking even the lowest place. It was faith that led him to God and lifted him up above all created things, making him search for happiness in the possession of God alone. Faith alone was his mistress, teaching him more than all the world's books.

43. It was faith that gave him this high regard for God, this great reverence for the sacred mysteries, especially for the most Blessed Sacrament of the altar where the Son of God resides like a King, and to which Lawrence was so devoted that he spent many hours, day and night, on his knees, rendering him homage and adoration. This same faith gave him a profound respect for the Word of God, for the Church and its holy ordinances, and for his superiors, whom he obeyed as the vicars of Jesus Christ. In fact, he believed the truths faith proposes to us with such certitude that he would often say, "None of the fine speeches I hear about God, nothing I read or experience myself can satisfy me, for God is infinite in his perfections, and consequently ineffable, so there are no words powerful enough to give me a perfect idea of his grandeur. Faith reveals him to me and lets me know him as he is. I learn more by this means in a short time than I would learn in school in many years." He would cry out, "O faith! O faith! O admirable virtue that illumines our minds and leads us to the knowledge of our Creator! Amiable virtue, how little known you are, and even less practiced, even though knowledge of you is so glorious and beneficial."

44. From this intense faith came the firmness of his hope in God's goodness, a filial trust in his providence, a total, universal surrender of himself into God's hands, without ever worrying about what would happen to him after his death. We will see this in greater detail when we speak of his inner dispositions during his last illness. It was not enough for him, for the greater part of his life, to rely on the grace and merits of Jesus Christ for his salvation. Rather, he forgot himself and his own interests entirely and, in the words of the Prophet,[31] threw himself headlong into the arms of infinite mercy. The more desperate things appeared, the more he hoped, like a rock that when beaten by the waves of the sea becomes a refuge in

the midst of the storm. We already saw this when we spoke of the inner struggles God sent him to test his fidelity soon after his entrance into religious life. If, as St. Augustine says, the measure of hope determines the measure of grace,[32] we can say that the grace God communicated to Brother Lawrence enabled him, as Scripture says, to hope against hope.[33] That is why he said the greatest glory you could give God was to completely mistrust your own strength and trust completely in his protection, because that is how to make a sincere confession of your own weakness and a true acknowledgment of the omnipotence of the Creator.

45. Love is the queen and soul of all the virtues, giving them of necessity their value and worth. We must not be surprised that the virtues possessed by Brother Lawrence were perfect, because the love of God reigned so perfectly in his heart, which, as St. Bernard said,[34] he had turned toward this divine object in all his affections. If faith enabled him to see God as sovereign truth, and if hope enabled him to contemplate God as his last end and ultimate happiness, love enabled him to recognize God as the most perfect of all beings or, more accurately, as perfection itself. Far from loving God for his own profit, his love was so disinterested that he loved God even when there was no suffering to avoid or any reward to gain, wanting only the good and glory of God and making the accomplishment of God's holy will his paradise. We will see this again during the last moments of his illness when his spirit was so free, even until the last sigh, that he expressed the dispositions of his heart as if he were in perfect health.

46. The purity of his love was so great that he wished, were it possible, that God did not see the deeds he performed in his service, so as to do them exclusively for God's glory, without any recompense. He complained lovingly, telling his friends that God let nothing go by without immediately rewarding him a hundredfold, often giving him such great experiences and tastes of his divinity that they sometimes overwhelmed him, making him say, with his typical reverence and familiarity, "It's too much, Lord, it's too much for me! Please give these kinds of favors and consolations to sinners and to those who do not know you, to attract them by such means to your service. I have the happiness of knowing you by faith, and it seems to me that should suffice. But because I must refuse nothing

from so generous a hand as yours, I accept, my God, the favors you grant me and, after receiving them, I return them to you as you gave them to me. Please be kind enough to accept them, for you know well it is not your gifts I seek and desire, but you yourself, and I can settle for nothing less."

47. This purity of love and this indifference served only to enkindle his heart more and intensify the flames of this divine fire whose sparks sometimes manifested themselves outwardly. Even though he made all kinds of efforts to hide the great impulses of divine love burning within him, he was occasionally unable to stop their outpourings, and his face was often visibly aglow. But when he was alone he let the fullness of this fire act and cried out to God, "Lord, give more space and room to the faculties of my soul, so that I can give greater expression to your love, or sustain me by your omnipotence, for otherwise I will be consumed by the flames of your love."

48. While he was conversing with his brothers he would often turn to God, lamenting the time he had wasted in his youth: "Goodness ever ancient, ever new, too late have I loved you![35] Do not waste your time, brothers, you are young. Take advantage of the sincere confession I am making to you of my lack of concern for God's service during my early years. Devote all yours to his love! As for me, if I had known earlier, if someone had told me the things I am now telling you, I would not have delayed in loving him. Believe me and count as lost all the time not spent in loving God."

49. Since love of God and love of neighbor are one and the same practice, you can estimate his love for his neighbor by the love he had for God, convinced as he was of what Our Lord said in the gospel: that the least service rendered to the least of his brothers was rendered to him.[36] He took special care to serve them in all the offices he held, and especially when he was assigned to the kitchen where, providing what was needed for the friars' subsistence according to the poverty of their state, he took pleasure in pleasing them as if they were angels. He inspired love in all those who succeeded him in this task. He helped the poor in their need to the extent of his ability. He consoled them in their afflictions and guided them with his advice. He encouraged them to gain heaven at the same time that they worked to earn their living. In a few words, he did all

the good he could do for his neighbor and never hurt anyone. He became all things to everyone to save them all for God.[37]

50. As Saint Paul says: love is patient, it triumphs over all difficulties, and it suffers everything [38] for the sake of the beloved. Therefore we cannot doubt Brother Lawrence's patience in his infirmities, he who loved God so perfectly. In fact, in keeping with the thought of the same apostle, patience has this fine rapport with love: just as love is the bond of perfection,[39] so patience is a perfect work—*opus perfectum habet* [40]—and therefore no more is needed to convince us of the perfect state to which God raised Brother Lawrence. We will see that he practiced these two virtues during the very painful illnesses with which it pleased God to afflict him. For without even discussing here a kind of sciatic gout that made him limp and degenerated into an intensely painful ulcer on the leg that tormented him for nearly twenty-five years,[41] I limit myself mainly to three major illnesses God sent him during the last years of his life to prepare him for death and make him worthy of the reward destined for him.

51. The first two illnesses were devastating. Lawrence nonetheless endured them with admirable patience and maintained the same evenness of spirit in the midst of these sufferings that he had possessed when he was in the most vigorous health. In the first case, he gave evidence of a desire for death, for when speaking with the physician after his fever went down, he told him, "Ah, Doctor, your remedies have worked too well for me; you only delay my happiness!" In the second, he seemed to have no preference whatsoever. He remained completely indifferent regarding life and death, perfectly resigned to God's orders. Content to live as to die, he wanted only what would please his divine Providence to ordain.

52. I can testify that he gave signs of altogether extraordinary constancy, resignation, and joy during the third illness, the one that separated his soul from his body, uniting it with his Beloved in heaven. He received much consolation from this blessed moment when it finally arrived, because he had longed for it for so long. The sight of death that frightens and dismays the most hardy did not intimidate him at all. He regarded it with complete confidence, and you could even say he defied it. When he saw the poor bed prepared for him, having overheard one of his friends say "It's for you,

Brother Lawrence. It's time to depart," he replied, "It is true. There is my deathbed, but someone who does not expect it at all will follow me immediately." This is exactly what happened, just as he had predicted. Although this friar [42] was in perfect health, he became ill the next day and died the same day Brother Lawrence was buried,[43] and the following Wednesday he was buried in the same grave. It seems that love united these two fine brothers in life and did not want them separated at death, for there was no other place [for burial] but the common grave.

53. Four or five months previously Lawrence had told several persons he would die before the end of February. He wrote two letters, two weeks apart, to a Blessed Sacrament sister.[44] He brought the first one[45] to a close with these words: "Goodbye. I hope to see him soon." And the second letter, dated February 6,[46] the day before he became ill, concluded with these words: "Goodbye. I hope for the merciful grace of seeing him in a few days." The same day he took to his bed,[47] he said to a friar in whom he confided that the illness would not last long, and that he would depart from this world very soon. He was so sure of the day of his death that the next day, Friday, he spoke more precisely and told one of the friars he would die the following Monday. This is what happened.

54. But let us return to the constancy he showed during his illness, before noting the circumstances of his death and his last sentiments. His only remaining desire was to suffer something for the love of God, and this made him repeat what he had said many times during his life, that his only suffering was that he had none, and that he found comfort in the existence of purgatory, for there at least he would suffer something for the remission of his sins. He found a favorable opportunity for this, however, in this life, and he did not let it go by. He deliberately turned on his right side, knowing this would cause him pain, and he wanted to stay there to satisfy his ardent desire to suffer. The brother looking after him wanted to comfort him a bit, but Lawrence told him twice: "Thank you, Brother, but please let me suffer a little for the love of God." In this painful state he said fervently, "My God, I adore you in my sufferings! This is how I will suffer something for you. May I soon suffer and die with you!" Then he would often repeat these verses of Psalm 50: *Cor mundum crea in me, Deus; ne projicias me a facie tua; redde mihi laetitiam*

salutaris tui, etc. [Create a clean heart in me, O God; do not turn away your face from me but give me back the joy of your salvation].[48]

55. The pain he felt in this position because of a spot on his right side, the result of pleurisy, was so unusual that he undoubtedly would have died had not the infirmarian arrived just at the right moment. He recognized the problem and turned Lawrence immediately on his other side, thereby allowing him, by this change, to breathe more freely. He was so intent on suffering that it became his whole consolation. It appeared as if he never had a moment of discomfort even in the midst of his most intense suffering. His joy showed not only on his face but was even evident from his manner of speaking, thus making the friars who visited him inquire whether he really was suffering at all. "Pardon me," he said to them, "I am in pain; this spot on my side hurts me, but my spirit is content." "But Brother," they replied, "if God asked you to suffer these pains for the duration of ten years would you still be content?" "I would be," he said, "not only for that number of years but I would willingly consent to endure them until the day of judgment, if God wanted, and I would hope he would give me the grace to always remain resigned." Such was Brother Lawrence's patience at the beginning of, and during, his four-day illness.

56. His fervor increased as the hour approached for his departure from this world. His faith became more intense, his hope more firm, and his love more ardent. You can judge the intensity of his faith by his frequent exclamations indicating his particular esteem for this virtue: "O faith! O faith!" he would exclaim, thus expressing a great deal about its excellence in a few words. Penetrated by its grandeur and illumined by its light, he adored God endlessly and explained that this adoration took place naturally in him. He once told a friar he hardly believed any more in the presence of God in his soul because he could already see something of this intimate presence by means of this luminous faith.

57. The firmness of his hope was no less apparent. His courage was so great during this most frightening time that he said to one of his friends who was questioning him on this subject that he feared neither death, nor hell, nor God's judgments, nor all the devil's efforts. In fact Lawrence saw the devil coming and going

around his bed but he mocked him. Hearing these things was so edifying that they continued to question him. They asked him if he knew that it was a terrifying thing to fall into the hands of the living God,[49] because no matter who you are you cannot know for sure if you are worthy of love or hatred.[50] "I agree," he said, "but I would not want to know for fear of being vain." He was so abandoned that, forgetting himself and seeking God alone and the accomplishment of his will, he would say, "Yes, if it were possible to love God in hell, I wouldn't care if he put me there, for he would be with me, and his presence would turn it into paradise. I have abandoned myself to him, so he can do with me as he pleases."

58. If he so loved God during his life, he did not love him any less at his death. He made continuous acts of love, and when a friar asked him if he loved God with all his heart, he answered, "Ah! If I thought that my heart did not love God, I would tear it out right now."

59. His suffering increased visibly. He received the last sacraments joyfully, fully conscious and with all his faculties, up until his last sigh. Although they rarely left him alone for a moment, day or night, and he received all the help he could expect from the kindness of his brothers, they did afford him some privacy so he could take advantage of the last precious moments of life to reflect on the great grace God had just given him in the last sacraments. He used these moments wisely to ask God for the final perseverance of his holy love. A friar asked him what he was doing and what he was thinking about. "I am doing what I will do for all eternity: I am blessing God, I am praising God, I am adoring him, and I am loving him with my whole heart. Our whole vocation consists of this, brothers, to love and adore God without worrying about anything else." A friar recommended himself to his prayers and pressed him to ask God for the grace of a true spirit of prayer. Lawrence told him that he had to cooperate and to do his part to make himself worthy of it. These were the last sentiments of his heart.

60. The next day, Monday, February 12, 1691, at nine o'clock in the morning, fully conscious, without agony or convulsions, Brother Lawrence of the Resurrection died in the embrace of the Lord and offered his soul to God with the peace and tranquility of one asleep.

61. His death was like a gentle sleep enabling him to pass from this miserable life to a blessed one. And so, if we can conjecture about what follows death from the holy actions that preceded it, we can state that Brother Lawrence left this world laden with good deeds and merit. It is easy to conclude, and it can be rightly presumed, that his death was so precious before God that its reward followed closely. His lot is among the saints, and he now enjoys the vision of glory. His faith was rewarded by clear vision, his hope by possession, and his charity by consummated love!

NOTES

1. Cf. Is 50:2.

2. For "Nicolas Herman" and "Hériménil" (which Beaufort spells "Hérimini"), see General Introduction, p. xviii and p. xxxix, note 6.

3. When Nicolas Herman was young, Lorraine was an independent duchy, though French-speaking. Charles IV of Lorraine, Duke since 1624, frequently participated in the intrigues of other courts, and for this reason he lost his duchy several times. During the particularly troubled period of the Thirty Years' War—the "troubles" of which Beaufort spoke; the war, famine, and illness in Lorraine to which Louis de Sainte-Thérèse refers several times in his *Annales* (I: 190, 461, 465, 476; II: 28, 215, 405)—Louis XIII, King of France, occupied the region from 1631–1637, the period during which Nicolas Herman's military experiences took place, as EL 8–9 describes.

4. The troups of Lorraine, to which Lawrence belonged, fought against the French occupation. Duke Charles IV became the ally of the Austrian emperor.

5. A rather vague allusion to Bernard of Saxe-Weimar's army. Bernard had joined his army to that of the brilliant strategist Gustave-Adolphe, King of Sweden, who fought the imperial Austrian troops in Germany. At the death of the King in 1632, Bernard became chief of the entire "Swedish" army. But after his defeat at Nordlingen in 1634, the Swedes separated from him. However, in 1635 the Swedes and Germans met as allies of the French troops against the imperial troops. In 1635 Bernard, who had taken Alsace, fought with the French in Lorraine.

6. In 1635, Charles IV, Duke of Lorraine, made serious efforts to regain his states. On August 10, he reconquered the French at Rambervillers (which Beaufort spells "Rambervilliers"). "Rambervillers was defended by 700 troops garrisoned there. Having broken through the walls of the town, the Duke, Charles IV, made their defenders surrender" (Ferdinand des Robert, *Campagne de Charles IV, duc de Lorraine et de Bar, en Allemagne, en Lorraine et en Franche-Comté, 1634–1638* [Paris: Chapion-Nancy, Silot, 1883],

p. 128). Lawrence must have been wounded on this occasion. Charles withdrew without a struggle from Rambervillers on October 17, 1635 (*ibid.,* p. 197).

7. Rambervillers is located 35 kilometers from Hériménil.

8. Cf. 2 Cor 1:3.

9. His uncle Jean, his mother's brother, a native of Hériménil. Jean Majeur entered the Discalced Carmelites as a lay brother at the beginning of October, 1633. He took the name "Brother Nicolas of the Conception." He was professed in Paris on December 9, 1635, and died on February 20, 1652, in his nephew's monastery in Paris. He was the son of Nicolas Mayeur (the name is spelled here with a "y") and Suzanne Poirson. See *Catalogus chronologicus et historicus,* p. 218, no. 93, and also *Necrologium carmelitarum discalceatorum,* p. 31. The Discalced Carmelite friars already had many foundations in Lorraine: Nancy (1611), Pont-à-Mousson (1623), and Gerbéviller (1624), only ten kilometers from Hériménil. But there were also Discalced Carmelite nuns at Nancy (1618), Pont-à-Mousson (1627), and Saint Mihiel (1628). In the present context, we should note expecially the Carmelite nuns' stay at Lunéville, only four kilometers from Nicolas's village. In 1628 the nuns established themselves in Lunéville, and remained until 1635, when "not finding safety here during the wars that were unsettling Lorraine, they returned to Nancy" (Louis de Sainte-Thérèse, *Annales,* p. 461).

10. Note that he was a lay brother.

11. Although an allusion to Wis 1:1 is possible ("Seek the Lord with simplicity of heart"), Beaufort's reference to the Apostle suggests the influence of Eph 6:5 (or Col 3:22), where slaves are encouraged to obey their masters in Christ in simplicity of heart; and of 1 Cor 5:8, which celebrates the new Paschal lamb "in sincerity and truth."

12. See the General Introduction, p. xix, and Appendix I.

13. Reminiscent, in Beaufort's words, of the response of St. John of the Cross to the crucified Lord [who asked John what he wished]: "to suffer and be despised for you, Lord." See also EL 24.

14. Brother Lawrence made his profession of vows on August 14, 1642.

15. The Venerable John of Jesus and Mary advised the cook to find a place of devotion "in or near the kitchen," in his *Discipline claustrale* [Discipline in the Cloister] (Paris: Robert Fouet, 1622), part 2, chap. 17, p. 171. Devotion to Christ's scourging at the pillar was widespread in Carmel, and also inspired St. Teresa of Avila, who describes her conversion in terms that may have influenced Beaufort: "[This image] represented the much wounded Christ.... I felt so keenly aware of how poorly I thanked him for those wounds that, it seems to me, my heart broke. Beseeching him to strengthen me once and for all that I might not offend him, I threw myself down before him with the greatest outpouring of tears" (see *Life,* 9, 1). Yet the similarity of the descriptions should not invite any doubt about the basic historical accuracy of the facts narrated.

16. See the General Introduction, p. xli, note 26.

17. St. Gregory the Great, *Dialogues*, "Patrologia Latina" series, vol. 66, Bk. II, chap. 35, col. 200; or "Sources chrétiennes" series, vol. 260 (Paris: Cerf, 1979), p. 241: "For the soul that sees the Creator, all creation is insignificant."

18. These are not literal quotations; cf. the Introductory Note to the Eulogy, p. 4, note 1.

19. Cf. L 2. Around 1682–1683, Lawrence declared that, after "the first ten years" of religious life, he enjoyed the "actual presence of God...for more than thirty years." If the remaining years until his death in 1691 are added, we arrive at the "forty" years of which Beaufort speaks here. In L 1, from 1682, this state lasted "about thirty years"; in SM 21, "for forty years."

20. For example, L 2 ("a silent, secret conversation with God") and L 15 ("an intimate, humble, loving conversation with him").

21. Cf. SM 8.

22. The indication of a "period of about [thirty years]" is at first misleading, since in CN 18–19, dated September 28, 1666, Beaufort related that Lawrence was "in charge of" the kitchen "for fifteen years," and afterwards put in the "sandal shop." The most reasonable interpretation would be to consider these fifteen years as the period when he was responsible for the kitchen as the official cook. But we can presume that Brother Lawrence regularly helped in the kitchen during the first years of his religious life. Beaufort indicates that his superiors assigned him to "various tasks" (EL 20), and that later, even as a sandal maker, he continued to help out in the kitchen—peeling the vegetables, for example, and doing other menial tasks—especially on feast days. Beaufort, who would not have had contact with Lawrence during his "fifteen years" as principal cook, nevertheless reports a comment from Lawrence about "flipping his little omelette in the frying pan" (M 10)!

23. That of sandal maker; cf. preceding note.

24. See note 4 of L 1.

25. "Conferences" in the sense of spiritual conversations.

26. Cf. Eph 4:22–24; Col 3:9–10.

27. Cf. Mt 11: 25.

28. This could not have been Fénelon. It may have been Msgr. de Noailles, Bishop of Châlon-sur-Marne, whom Beaufort served as vicar general. See the General Introduction, p. xl, note 18.

29. Cf. Jer 32:17–19, freely quoted from the Vulgate.

30. Cf. Rm 1:17, as influenced by Hb 2:4.

31. Probably a vague allusion to the Vulgate version of Psalm 54:23: "Cast your cares upon the Lord, and he will care for you."

32. The computerized complete concordance of St. Augustine offers nothing helpful here. The adage is a familiar one, and may come from a pseudo-Augustinian work.

33. Cf. Rm 4:18.

34. The computerized complete concordance of St. Bernard likewise offers nothing helpful here. This may have come from a pseudo-Bernardian work, or a personal reminiscence of Bernard's commentaries on the Canticle of Canticles.

35. This well-known exclamation is from St. Augustine's *Confessions*, 10:27 ("Patrologia latina" series, 39, col. 795). [Note, however, that Augustine speaks of *"beauty* ever ancient, ever new."]

36. Cf. Mt 25:40.

37. Cf. 1 Cor 9:22.

38. Cf. 1 Cor 13:4–7.

39. Col 3:14.

40. Jas 1:4.

41. According to CN 17 (September 28, 1666), he was already "crippled in one leg," twenty-four and one-half months before his death.

42. This reference is to ·Brother Philibert des Anges (Guillaume Poirson), born in 1616 at Roelieures in Lorraine, professed on July 13, 1642 at Pont-à-Mousson, and died in Paris on February 13, 1691. See the *Catalogus chronologicus*, p. 218, no. 102. The *Constitutions* (II, 4, 1–3) permitted other monasteries as well to receive lay brothers [*frères convers*] as novices; thus, Philibert made his profession at Pont-à-Mousson [rather than at Paris]. Note that the name of the mother of Lawrence's uncle Jean was also *Poirson*. We know that they both came from Lorraine. This raises the question of whether Lawrence and Philibert were related.

43. Lawrence was buried on February 13, 1691, the day after his death.

44. The Daughters of the Blessed Sacrament, whose convent garden bordered the property of the Discalced Carmelites. See Appendix I.

45. L 15.

46. L 16.

47. Thursday, February 8, 1691, as the rest of the text indicates.

48. Ps 51 (50): 12–14. All the religious know this psalm by heart, for it was often recited in common in Latin.

49. Cf. Heb 10:31.

50. Cf. Eccl 9:1 (in the Vulgate).

II

SPIRITUAL MAXIMS

Introductory Note
to the Spiritual Maxims

Here are texts from Brother Lawrence's own hand in his simple, direct style. The reader will soon discover his astounding contemplative depth once past the first chapter [1]—the only one that presents a problem, as we will see.

The pages of this little spiritual treatise as he presents it to us form a coherent whole. Following the general counsels to "undertake the spiritual life" (chapter 1), Lawrence moves on to the "practices," which are reduced in the concrete to the one "Practice," the "holiest, the most necessary" (SM 6): that of the presence of God who penetrates our entire life to the point of making it a prolonged adoration (chapter 3) and an actual union (chapter 4). He takes up the theme again and expands it (chapters 5–7), providing us with marvelous pages describing radiant contact with God. Lawrence communicates his own experience to us in a scarcely disguised autobiographical passage. The work concludes with the development of the three theological virtues with which it began (SM 1), thus completing the circle.

It is this beginning, our first chapter, that poses a problem from a critical point of view. Here we find what the fourth conversation (CN 51–54), chronologically earlier, already reported. The text of SM 1–5 is more extensive, but several sentences are literally identical; you need only compare them.[2] It is impossible that Brother Lawrence, even if he were treating themes so fundamentally dear to him, would write sentences—in the same order!—that were literally identical to those Beaufort recorded at the completion of a conversation, "as soon as I had left him" (SM 2).

Two hypotheses are possible. This first chapter may be from the hand of Brother Lawrence, and Beaufort, while editing the *Ways* in 1694, may have chosen some sentences (about half the chapter) to fill out his fourth conversation in 1667. On the other hand, here for the first chapter Beaufort may have drawn from his own notes of the *Conversations*, embellishing them with some new sentences that in fact sound quite "theological": he recalls *baptism*, the *glory of God* as the goal of our life, the necessity of *grace*, the habitual work of *Providence*, the *combat* between grace and the soul's three enemies. Although we cannot determine with absolute certitude, we opt for the second hypothesis. After all, it is unlikely that Beaufort would have omitted half of the completely sound sentences, as the first hypothesis would have us believe, if they were from Brother Lawrence.

This leads us to the question of the original manuscript of the *Maxims*. Was there a single manuscript as EL 2 suggests (a manuscript that bears the title: *Spiritual Maxims or means to acquire the presence of God* [3]), or several manuscripts, in the plural, as the title of the first book on Brother Lawrence [4] affirms? The second hypothesis seems the most probable to us. Chapter 3 could have been a reply to a question. Chapters 5–8 could have formed a special unit.[5] As for chapter 1, Beaufort could have elaborated on a page of notes from his fourth *Conversation*,[6] either by taking advantage of other separate thoughts of Brother Lawrence, or by personally developing—as we have conjectured above—some sentences in line with Brother Lawrence's convictions.

In any case, there is no reason to doubt that he maintained Lawrence's line of thought. Even if chronology or textual criticism are not his strong points, Beaufort is, nonetheless, an upright, discreet and faithful man. The vicar general, advisor, and confessor to Msgr. Noailles, is not a dreamer. Even though he has his own style—as we note in reading the *Eulogy*—the underlying reality of the biography fits in well with what we possess of the texts of Lawrence himself. Suzanne Boucheraux said it well: the biography is "of too pure a vein and the tone of the accounts too sincere for us to doubt the fidelity of a witness less concerned with describing the man than with conveying the words of a saint." [7]

It is in this spirit that we can welcome the few sentences that Beaufort probably added to Brother Lawrence's words in this first chapter. From there on we move into Lawrence himself in the style proper to this Carmelite whom we will get to know better in his *Letters*.

NOTES

1. That is to say, SM 1–5. We have obviously followed the order of texts that Beaufort's edition established, but we have introduced the caption "chapter" at the top, followed by its number, adding a title in brackets to chapter 1 only.

2. Cf. SM 1 and CN 51; SM 2 and CN 52; SM 3 and CN 53; SM 4 and the second half of CN 53; SM 5 and CN 54.

3. In the book, Beaufort only gives *Spiritual Maxims* as the general title of this section, with *Means to acquire the presence of God* as the title of the sixth unit, our chapter 6.

4. See the General Introduction, p. xxiv. The hypothesis of several manuscripts would agree more closely with expressions of EL 41: "some separate sheets," "some fragments."

5. Chapters 5 and 6, moreover, are linked by the words "Here are the means" (SM 26).

6. We will speak of this again in the Introductory Note to the *Conversations*, pp. 87–88.

7. In *L'Expérience*, p. 31.

Spiritual Maxims

CHAPTER 1

[PRINCIPLES]

1. Everything is possible for one who believes, still more for one who hopes, even more for one who loves, and most of all for one who practices and perseveres in these three virtues. All the baptized who are true believers have taken the first step along the way of perfection and will become perfect as long as they persevere in the practice of the following maxims.

2. We must keep our eyes fixed on God in everything we say, do or undertake. Our goal is to be the most perfect adorers of God in this life as we hope to be throughout all eternity. We must make a firm resolution to overcome, with God's grace, all the difficulties inherent in the spiritual life.

3. When we undertake the spiritual life we must seriously consider who we are, recognizing that we are worthy of all scorn, unworthy of the name Christian, and subject to all kinds of miseries and a multitude of setbacks. These disturb us and make our health, our moods, our inner dispositions and their outward manifestations changeable; in all, we are persons God wants to humble by means of a multitude of internal and external troubles and trials.

4. We must believe that it is advantageous for us and pleasing to God to sacrifice ourselves to him; that it is normal for his divine providence to abandon us to all sorts of trials, miseries and temptations for the love of God, and for as long as he likes. Without this submission of heart and mind to the will of God, devotion and perfection cannot endure.

5. A soul depends on grace in proportion to its desire for greater perfection. God's help is necessary at every moment because without it the soul can do nothing. The world, nature, and the devil[1] together wage war so fiercely and so relentlessly that, without this special help and this humble, necessary dependence, they would carry off the soul against its will. This seems contrary to nature, but grace finds pleasure and peace therein.

CHAPTER 2

PRACTICES NECESSARY TO ATTAIN THE SPIRITUAL LIFE

6. The holiest, most ordinary, and most necessary practice of the spiritual life is that of the presence of God. It is to take delight in and become accustomed to his divine company,[2] speaking humbly and conversing lovingly with him all the time, at every moment, without rule or measure, especially in times of temptation, suffering, aridity, weariness, even infidelity and sin.

7. We must continually apply ourselves so that all our actions, without exception, become a kind of brief conversation with God, not in a contrived manner but coming from the purity and simplicity of our hearts.

8. We must perform all our actions carefully and deliberately, not impulsively or hurriedly, for such would characterize a distracted mind. We must work gently and lovingly with God, asking him to accept our work, and by this continual attention to God we will crush the head of the devil and force the weapons from his hands.

9. During our work and other activities, even during our reading and writing, no matter how spiritual—and, I emphasize, even during our religious exercises and vocal prayers—we must stop for a moment, as often as possible, to adore God in the depths of our hearts, to savor him, even though in passing and stealthily.[3] Since

you are aware that God is present to you during your actions, that he is in the depths and center of your heart, stop your activities and even your vocal prayers, at least from time to time, to adore him within, to praise him, to ask his help, to offer him your heart, and to thank him. Nothing is more pleasing to God than to turn away from all creatures many times[4] throughout the day to withdraw and adore him present within. Moreover, this turning inward imperceptibly destroys the self-love found only among creatures. In the end, we can offer God no greater evidence of our fidelity than by frequently renouncing and scorning creatures in order to enjoy their Creator for a moment. I do not mean by this that you must withdraw forever from your duties,[5] for that would be impossible; prudence, the mother of all virtues, must be your guide. I do say, nonetheless, that it is a typical error among the spiritually minded not to withdraw from what is external from time to time to adore God within themselves and enjoy his divine presence in peace for a few moments. This digression was long but I thought the matter called for some explanation. Let's get back to our exercises.

10. All these adorations must be made by faith, believing that God is truly in our hearts, that we must adore, love, and serve him in spirit and in truth,[6] that he sees everything that happens and will happen in us and in all creatures; that he is independent of everything and the one on whom all creatures depend, infinite in every kind of perfection. He is the one who, by virtue of his infinite excellence and sovereign domain, deserves all that we are as well as everything in heaven and on earth, of which he can dispose as he wishes in time and in eternity. All our thoughts, words and actions belong by right to him. Let's put this into practice.

11. We must carefully examine which virtues are the most essential, which are the most difficult to acquire, which sins we commit most often, and which are the most frequent and inevitable of our falls. We must have recourse to God with complete confidence at the moment of combat, remain firm in the presence of his divine majesty, adore him humbly, bring him our miseries and weaknesses, and lovingly ask him for the help of his grace. In this way we will find every virtue in him without our having any of our own.

CHAPTER 3

HOW WE MUST ADORE GOD
IN SPIRIT AND IN TRUTH

12. This question contains three points to which we must respond. I say that adoring God in spirit and in truth[7] means adoring God as we are supposed to adore him.[8] God is spirit and we must adore him in spirit and in truth, that is, with humble, authentic adoration of spirit in the depths and center of our souls. God alone can see this adoration, which we can repeat so often that in the end it will become second nature to us, as if God were one with our souls and our souls were one with God. Practice will make this evident.

13. Adoring God in truth means recognizing him for what he is and recognizing ourselves for what we are. Adoring God in truth means recognizing truly, really, and in spirit that God is what he is, infinitely perfect, infinitely adorable, infinitely removed from all evil, and so on for all the divine attributes. Who are we, and what reason could excuse us from using all our strength to offer this great God all respect and adoration?

14. Adoring God in truth means admitting that, although we are completely opposite, he wants to make us like himself, if we so desire. We must not be so imprudent as to withhold, even for a moment, the respect, love, service and continual adoration we owe him.

CHAPTER 4

UNION OF THE SOUL WITH GOD

15. There are three kinds of union: the first is habitual, the second virtual, and the third actual.

16. Habitual union is when we are united to God solely by grace.

17. Virtual union is when we begin an action by which we are united with God and remain united with him by virtue of this action the entire time of its duration.

18. Actual union is the most perfect. And completely spiritual as it is, its movement is perceptible because the soul is not asleep[9] as in the other unions, but finds itself powerfully stirred. Its operation[10] is more intense than fire, more luminous than the sun in a clear sky. Nonetheless this feeling can be misleading, for it is not a simple expression of the heart, like saying "My God, I love you with all my heart," or other similar words.[11] It is, rather, an "I don't know what"[12] of the soul, gentle, peaceful, spiritual, respectful, humble, loving, and very simple,[13] that upholds and incites it to love God, to adore him, and even embrace him with an inexpressible tenderness that experience alone can enable us to understand.

19. Those who seek divine union must know that whatever attracts the will is in fact agreeable and delightful, or so it is perceived. We must admit that God is incomprehensible, and that to be united with him we must deprive the will of all sorts of spiritual and physical satisfactions so that, being thereby set free, it can love God above all things. If the will can in some respect comprehend God, it can do so only by love. There is a great difference between the tastes and sentiments of the will and the operations of the same will, because the tastes and sentiments of the will are in the *soul* as in their object [*terme*], and its operation, which is properly love, terminates in *God* as in its end.[14]

CHAPTER 5

ON THE PRESENCE OF GOD

20. The [practice of the] presence of God is an application of our mind to God, or a remembrance of God present, that can be brought about either by the imagination or the understanding.[15]

21. I know someone[16] who, for forty years,[17] has been practicing an intellectual presence of God to which he gives several other names. Sometimes he calls it a "simple act," a "clear and distinct knowledge of God," an "indistinct view" or a "general and loving awareness of God."[18] Other times he names it "attention to God" "silent conversation with God,"[19] "trust in God," or "the soul's life

and peace." This person told me that all these forms of God's presence are nothing but synonyms for the same thing, and that it is at present second nature to him. Here is how:

22. This person says that the habit is formed by the repetition of acts and by frequently bringing the mind back into God's presence. He says that as soon as he is free from his occupations, and often even when he is most taken up by them, the recesses of his mind [*esprit*] or the innermost depths of his soul are raised with no effort on his part and remain suspended[20] and fixed in God, above all things, as in its center and resting place. Since he is generally aware that his mind, thus held in suspension, is accompanied by faith, he is satisfied. This is what he calls "actual presence of God," which includes all the other types of presence and much more besides, so that he now lives as if only he and God were in the world. He converses with God everywhere, asks him for what he needs, and rejoices continuously with him in countless ways.

23. It is important, however, to realize that this conversation with God takes place in the depths and center of the soul. It is there that the soul speaks to God heart to heart, and always in a deep and profound peace that the soul enjoys in God. Everything that takes place outside the soul means no more to it than a lit straw that goes out as soon as it is ignited, and almost never, or very rarely, disturbs its inner peace.

24. To get back to the presence of God, I say that this gentle, loving awareness of God imperceptibly ignites a divine fire in the soul, inflaming it so intensely with love of God that one is forced to perform various activities in an effort to contain it.[21]

25. We would be surprised to know what the soul sometimes says to God, who is so pleased with these conversations that he grants it all its desires, providing it is willing to remain with him always, and in its center. To discourage the soul from returning to created things, God takes care to provide it with everything it desires, and to such an extent that it often finds within itself a very savory, delicious nourishment, though it never sought nor did anything to obtain it, and in no way contributed to it itself, except by its consent.

26. The presence of God is then the soul's life and nourishment, which can be acquired by the Lord's grace. Here are the means:

CHAPTER 6

MEANS TO ACQUIRE THE PRESENCE OF GOD

27. The first means is great purity of life.

28. The second is great fidelity to the practice of this presence and to the fostering of this awareness of God within, which must always be performed gently, humbly, and lovingly, without giving in to disturbance or anxiety.

29. We must take special care that this inner awareness, no matter how brief it may be, precedes our activities, that it accompanies them from time to time, and that we complete all of them in the same way. Since much time and effort are required to acquire this practice, we must not get discouraged when we fail, for the habit is only formed with effort, yet once it is formed we will find contentment in everything. It is only right that the heart, the first to beat with life and the part that controls the rest of the body, should be the first and the last to love and adore God, whether by beginning or by completing our spiritual and physical activities, and generally, in all life's exercises. This is the reason we must take care to foster this awareness, which we must do naturally and normally, as I have said, thus making it easier.

30. It would be appropriate for beginners to formulate a few words interiorly, such as: "My God, I am completely yours," or "God of love, I love you with all my heart," or "Lord, fashion me according to your heart," or any other words love spontaneously produces. But they must take care that their minds do not wander or return to creatures. The mind must be kept fixed on God alone, so that seeing itself so moved and led by the will, it will be obliged to remain with God.

31. This [practice of the] presence of God, somewhat difficult in the beginning, secretly accomplishes marvelous effects in the soul, draws abundant graces from the Lord, and, when practiced faithfully, imperceptibly leads it to this simple awareness, to this loving view of God present everywhere, which is the holiest, the surest, the easiest, and the most efficacious form of prayer.

32. Please note that to arrive at this state, mortification of the senses is presupposed, since it is impossible for a soul that still finds some satisfaction in creatures to completely enjoy this divine presence; for to be with God, we must abandon creatures.

CHAPTER 7

BENEFITS OF THE PRESENCE OF GOD

33. The first benefit that the soul receives from the [practice of the] presence of God is that its faith becomes more intense and efficacious in all life's situations, and especially in times of need, since it easily obtains graces in moments of temptation and in the inevitable dealings with creatures. For the soul, accustomed to the practice of faith by this exercise, sees and senses God present by a simple remembrance. It calls out to him easily and effectively, thus obtaining what it needs. It can be said that it possesses here something resembling the state of the blessed, for the more it advances, the more intense its faith grows, becoming so penetrating in the end that you could almost say: I no longer believe, for I see and experience.

34. The practice of the presence of God strengthens us in hope. Our hope increases in proportion to our knowledge. It grows and is strengthened to the extent that our faith penetrates the secrets of the divinity by this holy exercise, to the extent that it discovers in God a beauty infinitely surpassing not only that of the bodies we see on earth but even that of the most perfect souls and of the angels. The grandeur of the blessing that it desires to enjoy, and in some manner already tastes, satisfies and sustains it.

35. This practice inspires the will with a scorn for creatures, and inflames it with a sacred fire of love. Since the will is always with God who is a consuming fire,[22] this fire reduces to ashes all that is opposed to it. The soul thus inflamed can live only in the presence of its God, a presence that produces in its heart a holy ardor, a sacred zeal and a strong desire to see this God loved, known, served, and adored by all creatures.

36. By turning inward and practicing the presence of God, the soul becomes so intimate with God that it spends practically all its life in continual acts of love, adoration, contrition, trust, thanksgiving, oblation, petition, and all the most excellent virtues. Sometimes it even becomes one continuous act, because the soul constantly practices this exercise of his divine presence.

37. I know that few persons reach this advanced state. It is a grace God bestows only on a few chosen souls, since this simple awareness remains ultimately a gift from his kind hand. But let me say, for the consolation of those who desire to embrace this holy practice, that he ordinarily gives it to souls who are disposed to receive it. If he does not give it, we can at least acquire, with the help of ordinary grace, a manner and state of prayer that greatly resembles this simple awareness, by means of this practice of the presence of God.

NOTES

1. The three enemies of the soul, evoked (for example) by Saint John of the Cross in the *Counsels* and the *Precautions*. In the translation known to Lawrence, that of Cyprian of the Nativity (*Les Oeuvres spirituelles du b. père Jean de la Croix* [Paris: by the widow Chavalier, 1641]), nature is called "flesh" (pp. 339–340).

2. In thus insisting on the practice of the presence of God, Brother Lawrence certainly found support in the teachings of Saint Teresa of Avila, for example in the *Way of Perfection*, which was read each year in the refectory, especially chaps. 26 and 29 where the expression "to become accustomed to" recurs often: four times on p. 400 of the first volume of Cyprian's translation (Paris: Sebastian Hure, 1650), and five times on pp. 412–413.

3. This expression is found in a counsel of Venerable John of Jesus and Mary (*Discipline claustrale*, second part, 27:171) given to Carmelite cooks: to find a place near the kitchen where they could withdraw once they had prepared what was required, and where they offered, unnoticed, short prayers pleasing to God.

4. *Mille et mille*, "thousand and thousand," repeated shortly in SM 9, in this context means "frequently"; compare with SM 22, L 2 and L 16, where it means "many."

5. Could the manuscript of the *Maxims* found with the *Letters* be addressed to lay people? The counsel is appropriate for religious and laity alike. Lawrence would have understood the demands of their work (SM 9).

6. Cf. Jn 4:23.
7. Cf. Jn 4:23.
8. "God is spirit," etc. Jn 4:24.
9. "Asleep," meaning "unaware."
10. The context reveals that Lawrence is thinking of a mystical "operation" in which the soul, passively, "finds itself moved."
11. Useful expressions for beginners; see SM 30.
12. The expression "I don't know what" is taken from St. John of the Cross (*un no sé qué*). This is Cyprian's translation, for example, in the 7th strophe of the *Spiritual Canticle* (pp. 455ff.). The soul is wounded with love and knowledge of God.
13. This series of adjectives used to describe infused contemplation is reminiscent of similar series found in St. John of the Cross, e.g., "general, loving, peaceful, and tranquil knowledge" (*Ascent* 2, 14, 2); "this wisdom is loving, tranquil, solitary, peaceful, mild, and an inebriator of the spirit (*Flame* 3, 38); "loving knowledge, serene, peaceful, solitary" (*Flame* 3, 43)— a text that finds echoes in L 2 of Brother Lawrence.
14. To better understand this passage, which is Sanjuanist in tone, we have emphasized "soul" and "God."
15. Joseph de Sainte-Marie ("Lorenzo della Risurrezione: La vita nella presenza de Dio," *Rivista di vita spirituale* 39 [1985]: 454) points out here the probable influence of John of Jesus and Mary, who wrote in the *Instruction for Novices* that "the presence of God...is an application of the mind to God, conceived in an intellectual or imaginary manner" (pt. 4, chap. 3, p. 262). It is possible, however, that Brother Lawrence owes his definition to the oral teaching of his confreres or the reading of their works. In chapter ten of his *Abrégé de l'oraison mentale et la manière de s'y occuper longtemps et avec facilité* (Brussels, 1665), Cyprian of the Nativity wrote that "There are various types of the presence of God; one is formed by a sensible image called imaginary presence.... The other presence of God is called intellectual"; see *Études Carmélitaines* 20 (1935): 162.
16. The context clearly indicates that Brother Lawrence is speaking of himself.
17. "For forty years" is consistent with L 1 and 2 where Lawrence distinguishes between the first ten years of struggle and the following years when he lived peacefully and deeply in God; the formulation offers us a chronological indication, placing these pages around 1690.
18. Cf. L 2, note 6.
19. Cf. EL 29, note 20.
20. Cf L 2. This suspension is not ecstatic, however. Lawrence is wary of ecstasies, which he considers to be the trait of a soul "delighted by the gift" (CN 10).
21. Cf. L 1, note 4.
22. Cf. Heb 12:29.

III

LETTERS

Seventeenth-century engraving, by an unknown artist, of the church of Discalced Carmelite friars in Paris. (With permission of the Bibliothèque Nationale of Paris.)

Introductory Note
to the Letters

Compared to the *Eulogy,* it is a pleasure to read the sixteen letters in which Brother Lawrence reveals himself with the spontaneity and purity of an upright, free, very happy man who has now attained full maturity. The spiritual and the human coincide perfectly. Sometimes he inserts his own past and present experience in order to win his correspondents over to the practice of the presence of God.

Sixteen letters remain: one to a spiritual director (L 2), three to one or two laywomen (L 6, 9, 10), and the others to nuns. Out of discretion, one year after Brother Lawrence's death Beaufort replaced all the names with an *N.* (*Nomen,* name). To try to identify the various correspondents more precisely would only lead to very weak hypotheses.[1] We only know that some letters were addressed to a Carmelite nun (EL 28), and the last four letters were written to a "Daughter of the Blessed Sacrament."[2]

Of the sixteen letters, six are not dated. For reasons intrinsic to the texts we have changed the order of two of the letters.[3] In the end, the chronology is less important than the fact that the entire correspondence dates from the last ten years of Lawrence's life, when his doctrine was fully developed.

It is not surprising that the main theme of these letters is the search for, and the experience of, the presence of God. On several occasions Lawrence also addressed those who were suffering from physical problems. The remedies proved to be ineffective. Today when the powers of medicine are far greater, we would be less quickly convinced. The surrender that Lawrence—himself suffering, handicapped, ill—recommended to those who had tried the medicines of the period in vain, and who had furthermore vowed their lives to the Mystery of Christ and his church, proceeded from the mouth of a man who had personally overcome suffering. Lawrence of the Resurrection experienced suffering and submitted to it, but at the same time he governed and directed it. He transformed it into love. Suffering, personal imperfection, and emotional problems have never been satisfactorily explained, yet many saints have found in their faith in the living Christ the means to fill every void with Presence and love.

NOTES

1. The title "Reverend Mother" can refer to superiors of various congregations; furthermore, former prioresses and older sisters retained this title. When two *consecutive* letters are addressed to the same correspondent, Beaufort indicates this ("to the same"); thus we know that our L 3 and 4 are addressed to the same nun, and L 7 and 8 likewise to the same nun.

2. In EL 53, Beaufort quotes letters to "a Blessed Sacrament nun"; see note 1 of L 13. For L 14, 15 and 16 he indicates that they are addressed to the same person.

3. We will explain this in the notes for L 2 and L 9. The letters are given here in an order different from that of Beaufort, who put the first nine letters in this order: 1, 3, 4, 9, 2, 5, 6, 7, 8. After the tenth letter, the order is the same. [The salutations and closings of these letters has been adapted slightly to conform more closely with English style.]

Letters

LETTER 1

To a Nun

June 1, 1682

Reverend Mother,

I have taken advantage of this opportunity to share with you the experience of one of our friars[1] concerning the admirable effects and continual help he receives from the practice of the presence of God; we can both benefit from it.

You will see that his principal concern throughout the more than forty years he has been in religious life[2] has been always to be with God, and to do, say, or think nothing that could displease him. He has no other interest than the pure love of God who deserves infinitely more besides. He is now so accustomed to this divine presence that he receives constant help in every situation. His soul has been enjoying continual inner consolations for about thirty years.[3] Sometimes they are so intense he is forced to do childish things in order to control them and keep them from showing outwardly.[4] This behavior makes him look more foolish than holy!

If occasionally he becomes too forgetful of this divine presence, God makes himself known immediately in his soul to call him back to himself; this often happens when he is most engaged in his activities.[5] He responds with complete fidelity to this inner call: either by lifting up his heart toward God, by gently and lovingly turning inward, or by a few words that love formulates during these encounters, for example: "My God, I am all yours; Lord, fashion me according to your heart." It seems to him, in fact, that this God of love, satisfied with these few words, falls back to sleep[6] and rests in the depths and center of his soul. These experiences make him so certain that God is always in the depths of his soul, that he has no doubts about it, no matter what he may do or what may happen.

Judge for yourself, Reverend Mother, how great is the contentment and satisfaction he enjoys. Constantly perceiving so great a treasure within himself, he has no anxiety about finding nor any about seeking it; it is completely accessible, and he is free to make use of it as he pleases.

He often complains of our blindness and cries out ceaselessly that we are deserve sympathy for settling for so little. "God," he says, "has infinite treasures to give us, yet we are satisfied with a bit of perceptible devotion that passes in an instant." He complains that "we are blind since we bind God's hands in this way and halt the abundant flow of his graces; yet when God finds a soul penetrated by an intense faith he pours out his graces in abundance. This torrent of his grace, impeded from running its ordinary course, expands impetuously and abundantly once it has found an outlet."

Yes, sometimes we stop this torrent by our lack of appreciation for it. We must not stop it any longer, dear Mother; we must turn inward, break through the dam, let grace come forth, and make up for lost time. We have so little time left to live. Death is at our heels, so be on guard: death comes only once!

Once again, we must turn inward; time is flying, and there is no escape. Everyone is accountable for himself. I believe you have taken appropriate measures so that there will be no surprises; I praise you for it, for this is our concern. Nonetheless we must never stop working, since in the spiritual life, not to advance is to go backwards. Those who are empowered by the breath of the Holy Spirit sail along even when asleep. If the ship of our soul is still beaten by the winds or the storm, we must wake the Lord who is resting there, and he will immediately calm the sea.[7]

I have taken the liberty, dear Mother, to share these fine sentiments with you so you can compare them with your own; they will serve to rekindle and inflame yours, if unfortunately—contrary to God's will, for this would be a tragedy—they have become even slightly cold. Let us both recall the fervor we had when we began. Let us profit from the example and sentiments of this friar, little known in the world but known and caressed by God. I will ask this grace for you; earnestly ask the same for him who is in Our Lord, Reverend Mother,

Yours,

From Paris, June 1, 1682

NOTES

1. The Discalced Carmelite friar referred to here is obviously Lawrence himself, as the contents of the letter confirm.

2. Exactly forty-one years, ten and one-half months.

3. Cf. note 2 of L 2.

4. Cf. L 2 and 13; CN 36; SM 24; EL 36.

5. In spite of his seventy-two years of age, Lawrence is thus still active.

6. "Falls back to sleep" after God makes himself known to call Brother Lawrence back to his presence.

7. Cf. Mt 8: 23–27.

LETTER 2

To a Spiritual Director[1]

1682–1683 [2]

Dear Reverend Father,

Since I am not able to find my way of life described in books—although this does not really disturb me—I would, nonetheless, like to have the reassurance of knowing your thoughts on my present state.

Several days ago during a discussion with a pious person, I was told the spiritual life was a life of grace that begins with servile fear, that intensifies with the hope of eternal life, and that finds its consummation in pure love; and that there are various ways of ultimately arriving at this blessed consummation.

I haven't followed these methods at all; on the contrary, I don't know why they provoked such fear in me in the beginning. But for this reason, on my entrance into religious life I made the resolution to give myself entirely to God in atonement for my sins, and to renounce everything else for the sake of his love.

During the first years I ordinarily thought about death, judgment, hell, paradise, and my sins when I prayed. I continued in this fashion for a few years,[3] carefully applying myself the rest of the day—even during my work—to the practice of the presence of God who was always near me, often in the very depths of my heart. This gave me a great reverence for God, and in this matter faith alone was my reassurance.

I gradually did the same thing during mental prayer, and this gave me great joy and consolation. This is how I began. I will admit that during the first ten years I suffered a great deal. The apprehension that I did not belong to God as I wished, my past sins always before my eyes, and the lavish graces God gave me, were the sum and substance of all my woes. During this period I fell often, but I got back up just as quickly. It seemed to me that all creatures, reason, and God himself were against me,[4] and that faith alone was on my side. I was sometimes troubled by thoughts that this was the result of my presumption, in that I pretended to be all at once where others were able to arrive only with difficulty. Other times I thought I was willingly damning myself, that there was no salvation for me.

When I accepted the fact that I might spend my life suffering from these troubles and anxieties—which in no way diminished the trust I had in God and served only to increase my faith—I found myself changed all at once. And my soul, until that time always in turmoil, experienced a deep inner peace as if it had found its center and place of rest.[5]

Since that time I do my work in simple faith before God, humbly and lovingly, and I carefully apply myself to avoid doing, saying, or thinking anything that might displease him. I hope that, having done all that I can, he will do with me as he pleases.

I cannot express to you what is taking place in me at present. I feel neither concern nor doubt about my state since I have no will other than the will of God, which I try to carry out in all things and to which I am so surrendered that I would not so much as pick up a straw from the ground against his order, nor for any other reason than pure love.

I gave up all devotions and prayers that were not required and I devote myself exclusively to remaining always in his holy presence. I keep myself in his presence by simple attentiveness and a general loving awareness of God[6] that I call "actual presence of God" or better, a quiet and secret conversation of the soul with God that is lasting. This sometimes results in interior, and often exterior, contentment and joys so great that I have to perform childish acts, appearing more like folly than devotion,[7] to control them and keep them from showing outwardly.

Therefore, Reverend Father, I cannot doubt at all that my soul has been with God for more than thirty years. I will omit a number of things so as not to bore you. I think, however, it would be appropriate to indicate the manner in which I see myself before God, whom I consider as my King.

I consider myself as the most miserable of all human beings, covered with sores, foul, and guilty of all sorts of crimes committed against my King[8]; moved by sincere remorse I confess all my sins to him. I ask him pardon and abandon myself into his hands so he can do with me as he pleases. Far from chastising me, this King, full of goodness and mercy, lovingly embraces me, seats me at his table, waits on me himself, gives me the keys to his treasures, and treats me in all things as his favorite; he converses with me and takes delight in me in countless ways, without ever speaking of forgiveness or taking away my previous faults. Although I beg him to fashion me according to his heart, I see myself still weaker and miserable, yet ever more caressed by God. This is what I see from time to time while in his holy presence.

My most typical approach is this simple attentiveness and general loving awareness of God, from which I derive greater sweetness and satisfaction than an infant receives from his mother's breast. Therefore, if I may dare use the expression, I would gladly call this state the "breasts of God,"[9] because of the indescribable sweetness I taste and experience there.

If on occasion I turn away either because of necessity or weakness, inner movements[10] so charming and delightful that I am embarrassed to talk about them, call me immediately back to him. I beg you, Reverend Father, to think about my great weaknesses, of which you are fully aware, rather than these great graces with which God favors my soul, unworthy and ignorant as I am.

Regarding the prescribed hours of prayer, they are nothing more than a continuation of this same exercise. Sometimes I think of myself as a piece of stone before a sculptor who desires to carve a statue; presenting myself in this way before God I ask him to fashion his perfect image in my soul, making me entirely like himself.[11]

At other times, as soon as I apply myself I feel my whole mind and soul raised without trouble or effort, and it remains suspended and permanently rooted in God as in its center and place of rest.

I know that some would call this state idleness, self-deception, and self-love. I maintain that it is a holy idleness and a blessed self-love, should the soul in this state be capable of it. In fact, when the soul is in this state of rest its former acts do not trouble it; these acts were formerly its support but now they would do more harm than good.

I cannot agree to calling this self-deception, since the soul in this state desires God exclusively. If this is self-deception then it is up to God to correct it; may he do with me as he pleases, for I seek him alone and want to be entirely his. I would appreciate it if you would let me know your impressions of this. It would mean a great deal to me for I have a special regard for you, Reverend Father, and am, in Our Lord,

Yours,

NOTES

1. This "Father" could be a Carmelite from another monastery—the reason Lawrence wrote and waited for the priest's reply—or a priest from another Congregation. In any event, he was well aquainted with Brother Lawrence ("you know well my miseries"). This letter qualifies somewhat, at least for the later period, an annotation of Beaufort in 1666 (CN 21–22, evoked again in W 21), according to which Lawrence had no "director" but only a "confessor" to receive absolution for his sins. He occasionally consulted the priest of L 2, to whose judgment "he always deferred."

2. This letter has no date but evokes "the first ten years of his religious life," which all of a sudden is changed into a profound peace that, from that time, "lasted more than thirty years." Written some forty years since his entrance in June 1640, we propose this approximate date [for the letter], before L 4 of November 3, 1685. Cf. note 7 as well.

3. Cf. CN 24: "In the beginning, however, he meditated discursively for some time."

4. There may be an influence from St. John of the Cross here on the level of the description. The soul "feels very vividly indeed the shadow of death, the sighs of death, and the sorrows of hell, all of which reflect the feeling of God's absence, of being chastised and rejected by him.... Such persons also feel forsaken and despised by creatures, particularly by their friends," and "that this affliction will last forever" (*Night* 2, 6, 2–3). "It seems God is against them," and "the soul understands clearly that it is worthy neither of God nor of any creature" (*Night* 2, 5, 5).

5. The following note reveals that Brother Lawrence used the terminology of his spiritual father in Carmel, St. John of the Cross, to describe his spiritual experiences, and this is to be expected. John of the Cross often spoke of the "center" where the soul remains "in loving awareness of God, without particular considerations, in *interior peace* and quiet and *repose*" (*Ascent* 2, 13, 4); we have emphasized here the words also found in Lawrence.

6. Cf. St. John of the Cross, *Ascent* 2, 13, 6 ("general loving awareness"); *Ascent* 2, 14, 2 ("general loving knowledge"); *Ascent* 2, 14, 6 ("the loving general knowledge or awareness of God"); *Ascent* 2, 14, 12, ("general loving knowledge"). In *Flame* 3, 33-34, John speaks of a "loving attention to God" involving a "*simple* loving awareness" (note Lawrence's use of the word "simple"), in contrast to the discursive work of the intellect.

7. See L 1, note 4. The reader will note that the last six lines are found, almost word for word, in L 1. This may indicate a chronological proximity with the letter of June 1, 1682.

8. It should be noted that this was the period of "Kings," specifically Louis XIV in France.

9. Inspired by Song 8:1, St. John of the Cross uses the image of breasts to symbolize the passions (*Canticle* 22, 7; 24, 5) or reasoning (*Night* 1, 9,9), or creatures in general (*Night* 2, 23, 12), which must be renounced for the sake of "divine touches" and "loving awareness." In *Canticle* 27, 3-5, "to give one's breast" has an entirely mystical meaning. It is God's communication of "his love and secrets," a "sweet and living knowledge," "secret" and passive.

10. Cf. L 1, note 6.

11. John of the Cross uses the comparison of a statue before its sculptor, but in the context of community life (*Precautions* 15; *Counsels* 3). The theme of "resemblance" is an important one to the saint.

12. The terminology of the following passage reflects the *Flame* of St. John of the Cross (3, 44–45), in which the unenlightened spiritual director objects, stating that such idleness is a waste of time. "Since hammering with the faculties is this director's only teaching, ...he will say: 'Come, now, lay aside these rest periods, which amount to idleness and a waste of time; take and meditate and make interior acts...; this other method is the way of illusions and typical of fools.' Thus, not understanding the stages of prayer or the ways of the spirit, these directors are not aware that these acts they say the soul should make...are already accomplished."

LETTER 3

To a Nun[1]

1685[2]

Reverend and Dear Mother,

Today I received two books and a letter from Sister *N.*, who is preparing for her profession of vows, and who, for that reason, asks for the prayers of your community and for yours in particular.[3] She strikes me as having a great and singular trust, so do not disappoint her, but pray that she may make her sacrifice for the sake of God's love alone and with a firm resolution to be completely his. I will send you one of these books that treat of the practice of the presence of God. This is, in my opinion, the essence of the spiritual life, and it seems to me that by practicing it properly you become spiritual in no time.

I know that to do this your heart must be empty of all other things because God desires to possess it exclusively, and he cannot possess it exclusively without first emptying it of everything other than himself; neither can he act within it nor do there what he pleases.

There is no way of life in the world more agreeable or delightful than continual conversation with God; only those who practice and experience it can understand this. I do not suggest, however, that you do it for this reason. We must not seek consolations from this exercise, but must do it from a motive of love, and because God wants it.

If I were a preacher, I would preach nothing but the practice of the presence of God; and if I were a spiritual director, I would recommend it to everyone, for I believe there is nothing so necessary or so easy.

Ah! If we only knew how much we needed God's graces and help, we would never lose sight of him, not even for a moment. Believe me and make a holy and firm resolution at once never to deliberately turn away from him, and to live the rest of your life in this holy presence, deprived for his love of all the consolations of heaven and earth, should he so judge. Put your hand to the plough; if you carry this out properly you can rest assured you will soon see the benefits. I will help you with my prayers, poor as they are. I commend myself fervently to yours and to those of your holy community. My regards to all and to you especially,

Yours,

NOTES

1. This letter is not addressed to the same nun as L 1, for otherwise Beaufort would have put, according to his custom, the indication "to the same," as in his own edition where L 1 and L 3 follow each other.

2. Approximate date deduced from L 4 (of November 3, 1685), where Lawrence expressed his astonishment at not receiving a reaction to the subject of the "book" he sent.

3. Still a novice, this nun is from another Congregation than the recipient whose prayers she asks through Brother Lawrence.

LETTER 4

To the Same Nun[1]

November 3, 1685

Reverend and Dear Mother,

I received from Miss *N*. the rosaries that you gave her. I am surprised you haven't let me know what you think of the book I sent you. You must have received it. Put it diligently into practice in your later days. Better late than never.

I cannot understand how religious people can remain content without the practice of the presence of God. As for me, I keep myself recollected in him in the depth and center of my soul as much as possible, and when I am thus with him I fear nothing, though the least deviation is hell for me.

This exercise does not hurt the body. It is nonetheless appropriate to deprive it occasionally, and even with some frequency, of some innocent, permissible, little consolations. For God will not permit a soul desirous of being entirely his to find consolation other than with him, and that is more than reasonable!

I do not say we must put ourselves to a great deal of trouble to do this; no, we must serve God in holy freedom. We must work faithfully, without turmoil or anxiety, gently and peacefully bringing our minds back to God as often as we find ourselves distracted.

We must, however, place all our trust in God and let go of all our cares, including a multitude of private devotions, very good in themselves but often carried out for the wrong reason, for these devotions are nothing more than the means to arrive the end. If, then, we are with the one who is our end by this practice of the presence of God, it is certainly useless to return to the means. We can continue our loving exchange with him, remaining in his holy presence sometimes by an act of adoration, praise, or desire, other times by acts of oblation, thanksgiving, or anything else that our minds can devise.

Do not be discouraged by the repugnance you feel on the side of nature. You must do it violence. In the beginning you may often think you are wasting your time; nonetheless, you must continually resolve to persevere until death in spite of all the difficulties. I commend myself to the prayers of your holy community and to yours in particular and I am in Our Lord,

Yours,

From Paris, November 3, 1685

NOTE

1. Beaufort deliberately indicated "to the same" person as the previous letter. The contents (the "book" on the presence of God) confirm this; cf. L 3, note 2.

LETTER 5

To a Nun

[no date]

Reverend and Dear Mother,

My prayers, though of little worth, are with you as I promised[1]; I will keep my word. How happy we would be if we could only find the treasure of which the gospel speaks[2]; nothing else would matter. Since it is inexhaustible, the more we search, the more riches we find.[3] Let us devote ourselves ceaselessly to looking for it; let us not grow weary until we have found it....[4]

Finally, Mother, I do not know what will become of me. It seems to me that peace of mind and soul comes to me in my sleep.[5] Even if I were capable of suffering, it would be from not having any suffering at all; and if God permitted it, purgatory, where I believe I could suffer in atonement for my sins, would be a consolation to me. I only know that God looks after me. My tranquility is so great that I fear nothing. What could I fear when I am with him? I cling to him with all my strength. May he be blessed by all. *Amen.*[6]

Yours,

NOTES

1. Promises of prayer in L 1 and L 3. The recipient is probably the same as in L 3, but Beaufort could not indicate "to the same" in every instance, since in his series our Letter 2 is placed between L 3 and L 5.

2. Cf. Mt 13:44.

3. Lawrence describes the "treasure" as extremely vast, into which one can search. He probably owes this elaboration of the gospel image to St. John of the Cross who, in his *Canticle* 37, 4, wrote on the subject of the infinite mystery of Christ, who "is like an abundant mine with many recesses of

treasures, so that however deep individuals may go they never reach the end or bottom, but rather in every recess find new veins with new riches everywhere."

4. The text is cut here, and Beaufort explains that "He referred here to some specific incidents and then later said: ...."

5. A probable allusion to Ps 127 (126):2: "He gives to his Beloved in sleep."

6. "May He be blessed by all. *Amen*": An exclamation that recurs in L 9 and L 12, and that Brother Lawrence could have often read, or heard read, from St. Teresa's *Works*.

LETTER 6

To a Woman

October 12, 1688

Dear Madame,

Our God is infinitely good and knows what we need. I have always known he would bring you low. He will come to raise you up in his own time, and when you least expect it. Hope in him more than ever. Join me in thanking him for the graces he gives you, especially for the strength and patience he gives you in your afflictions. This is an obvious sign of his care for you. Find consolation in him and thank him for everything.

I also admire the strength and courage of Mr. *N.*[1] God has given him a pleasant disposition and good will, but he is still a bit worldly and rather inexperienced. I hope the affliction God sent him will serve as an effective medicine, and that it will bring him to his senses. This is an opportunity for him to place all his trust in God who is always with him. May he think of him as much as possible, especially in times of greatest danger.

A brief lifting up of the heart is enough. A brief remembrance of God, an act of inner adoration—even though on the run with sword in hand—these prayers, short as they may be, are pleasing to God[2] and, far from causing those engaged in battle to lose courage in the most dangerous circumstances, fortify them. May he think of this as often as possible so that he becomes gradually accustomed to this simple yet holy exercise; no one sees it, and there is nothing easier than to repeat these little inner adorations frequently throughout the day. Please recommend that he remember God as often as possible in the manner indicated here. It is very appropriate and necessary for a soldier who is always exposed to threats to

his life and often to his salvation. I hope God will help him and his whole family to whom I send my regards, and I am yours,
    Most humbly,

October 12, 1688

NOTES

1. As the reader will see, Lawrence is referring to a young soldier. He speaks of "dangers," "weapons," a "sword," etc.
2. Reminiscent of Venerable John of Jesus and Mary; cf. note 3 of SM 9.

LETTER 7

To a Nun

[no date]

Reverend and Dear Mother,

You are telling me nothing new, and you are not the only one who experiences distractions. The mind is extremely flighty, but the will, mistress of all our powers, must take hold of it and bring it back to God as to its final end.

If the mind has not been disciplined early on, it can easily become distracted and dissipated, in which case these harmful tendencies will ordinarily drag us down to earthly things in spite of all our efforts, for they are difficult to overcome.

I think the answer to our problems is to confess our faults and to humble ourselves before God. I advise you against long discourses during mental prayer, for they often foster distractions. Remain before God like a poor, mute paralytic at the door of a rich man. Strive to be attentive to God's presence. If your mind wanders or withdraws occasionally, don't get upset. Since these disturbances tend to distract the mind rather than focus it, we must use the will to gently collect our thoughts. If you persevere in this manner God will have mercy on you.

An easy way to keep the mind from wandering during the time of mental prayer is to keep it as still as possible—not to let it take flight—during the day. You must keep it faithfully in God's presence; and once you are accustomed to think of him from time to time, it will be easy to remain calm during prayer, or at least to bring the mind back when it wanders.

I have spoken to you at length in my other letters[1] of the advantages to be gained from this practice of the presence of God. Let us devote ourselves to it seriously and pray for each other. I commend myself to the prayers of Sister *N.* and of Reverend Mother *N.* and I am yours in Our Lord,

Very humbly,

NOTE

1. The reference may be to L 3 and L 4, or else to lost letters, or to the manuscript of the *Spiritual Maxims* found among the letters (see General Introduction, p. xxiii).

LETTER 8

TO THE SAME NUN[1]

March 28, 1689

Here is my reply to Sister *N.*'s letter; kindly take the trouble to give it to her. It seems like her heart is in the right place, but she wants to advance faster than grace would allow. You don't become a saint in a day![2] I entrust her to you, for we must help each other with advice and even more so by our good example. I would greatly appreciate it if you would let me know from time to time how she is doing, and if she is indeed fervent and obedient.

Let us often recall, dear Mother, that our only concern in this life is to please God, and that everything else is folly and vanity. We have spent more than forty years in religious life.[3] Have we used them to love and serve God who in his mercy has called us to this? I am filled with shame and embarrassment when I consider how, on the one hand, God ceaselessly gives me such great graces, and how, on the other, I make such poor use of them and fail to profit from them along the way of perfection.

Since in his mercy he still gives us a little time, let's take advantage if it! We can make up for lost time and return to this Father of goodness with complete trust. He is always ready to receive us lovingly. Let us renounce, dear Mother, and renounce completely for the sake of his love all that is not God; he deserves infinitely more. Let us think of him continually. Let us put all our trust in him, for I have no doubt that we will soon reap the benefits and know the abundance of his grace, with which we can do everything and without which we can only sin.

It is impossible to avoid the dangers and hazards which life is full of without God's actual, constant help; let us ask him for it continually. We cannot ask him for it unless we are with him. We cannot be with him unless we think of him often. We cannot think of him often unless we habitually practice this holy exercise. You will tell me that I always say the same thing. It is true. I know no other means more appropriate or easier than that! And since I practice no other, I recommend it to everyone. We must know before we can love. To know God we must think of him often. And when our love is strong we will think of him very often for our heart will be where our treasure is.[4] Think about this often and think about this carefully!

Your very humble,

NOTES

1. Beaufort's indication: "to the same."

2. A young nun who "wanted to advance faster than grace would allow," but who is not necessarily the same one "preparing for profession" in L 3.

3. At that time (i.e., the date of the letter) Lawrence had spent nearly 49 years "in religion," but he takes on the perspective of his correspondent.

4. Mt 6:21.

LETTER 9

To a Woman

[around 1689]¹

Dear Madame,

I truly feel sorry for you; if you could entrust your concerns to Mr. and Mrs. *N.* and concern yourself only with God, you would win a great victory! God does not ask a great deal of us: a brief remembrance from time to time, a brief act of adoration, occasionally to ask him for his grace or offer him your sufferings, at other times to thank him for the graces he has given you and is giving you. In the midst of your work find consolation in him as often as possible. During your meals and conversations, occasionally lift up your heart to him; the least little remembrance of him will always be most agreeable. You need not shout out²: he is closer to us than we may think.

We do not always have to be in church to be with God. We can make of our hearts an oratory where we can withdraw from time to time to converse with him there, gently, humbly, and lovingly. Everyone is capable of these familiar conversations with God, some more, some less. He knows what we can do. Let's try. Perhaps he is only looking for the right intention on our part. Courage, we have only a short time left to live: you are nearly sixty-four and I am almost eighty. Let us live and die with God. Sufferings will always be sweet and pleasant when we are with him, and without him the greatest pleasures are cruel punishment. May he be blessed by all. *Amen.*

Gradually become accustomed³ to adoring him in this way, asking him for his grace, offering him your heart from time to time, during the day, while at work, at every possible moment. Do not force yourself to follow special rules or practice private devotions; do this in faith, with love and humility.

You can assure Mr. and Mrs. *N.* and Miss *N.* of my poor prayers, and that I am their servant and particularly yours, in Our Lord,

Brother,

NOTES

1. This undated letter, which Beaufort inserted in fourth place, after that of November 3, 1685 (our L 4), has been placed here with the approximate date of 1689, since Lawrence said he was approaching 80 years of age. In 1685 he would have only been 71; in 1689 he was at least 75.

2. Cf. St. Teresa of Avila, *Way* 9, 5: "It isn't necessary to shout in order to speak to [God], for His Majesty will give the experience that he is present [within]."

3. "To become accustomed to," an expression dear to St. Teresa of Avila; cf. SM 6, note 2.

LETTER 10

To a Woman

October 29, 1689

Dear Madame,

I really had a lot of trouble getting myself to write to Mr. *N.* I am only doing it because you and Mrs. *N.* want me to. Please be kind enough to address and mail this. I am indeed content with the trust you have in God; I hope he will increase it more and more. We cannot have too much trust in so good and faithful a friend, who will never fail us in this world or the next.

If only Mr. *N.* knew how to profit from the loss he has suffered and would place all his trust in God, he would soon give him another more powerful and better-intentioned friend, for God disposes hearts as he pleases. Perhaps his affection for and attachment to the friend he lost were too great; we must love our friends but without prejudice to the love of God, which must come first. Remember, I beg you, what I recommended to you,[1] that is, to think of God often, night and day, in all your activities, and even when you relax. He is always near you and with you; do not leave him alone. You would consider it rude to leave a friend who is visiting you by himself; then why abandon God and leave him alone? Do not forget him. Think of him often, adore him continually, live and die with him. This is the true occupation of a Christian; in a word, this is our trade. If we don't know it, we must learn it! I will help you with my prayers. I am in Our Lord,

Yours,

From Paris, October 29, 1689

NOTE

1. Perhaps in L 9; in that case L 9 and L 10 are addressed to the same person. It is possible that the "recommendation" to live in the presence of God was made in an oral conversation or in a lost letter.

LETTER 11

To a Nun

November 17, 1690

Reverend and Dear Mother,[1]

I will not ask God to deliver you from your trials, but I will ask him earnestly to give you the patience and strength needed to suffer as long as he desires. Find consolation in him who keeps you fixed to the cross[2]; he will release you when he judges it appropriate. Happy are they who suffer with him. Get used to suffering, and ask him for the strength to suffer as he wants, and for as long as he judges necessary. The worldly do not understand these truths, and I am not surprised; the reason is that they suffer as citizens of this world and not as Christians. They consider illnesses as natural afflictions and not as graces from God, and therefore they find in them only what is difficult and harsh for [our] nature. But those who regard them as coming from the hand of God, as signs of his mercy and the means he uses for their salvation, ordinarily find great sweetness and perceptible consolations in them.

I wish you were convinced that God is often closer to us in times of sickness and suffering than when we enjoy perfect health. Seek no other doctor but him. I think he wants to cure you by himself. Place all your trust in him, and you will soon experience the benefits we resist when we trust more in [medical] remedies than in God.

Whatever remedies you may use, they will only work to the extent that he will permit. When suffering comes from God, he alone can cure it, and he often leaves us with physical illness in order to cure our spiritual illness. Find consolation in the sovereign doctor of body and soul.

I can anticipate your reply, that I have it easy since I eat and drink at the Lord's table. You are right. But you must realize my suffering is not insignificant, for I am the greatest criminal in the world, and yet I eat at the King's table, and am served by his hands, without the assurance of his pardon. My great distress is lessened only by my trust in the goodness of my Sovereign Lord. Therefore I assure you, whatever enjoyment I may find eating and drinking at my King's table, my sins, always present before my eyes, as well as the lack of certitude concerning my forgiveness,[3] torment me nonetheless; though truthfully, the suffering is agreeable....

Be content with the state in which God has placed you; no matter how happy you may think I am, I envy you. Such pains and sufferings would be paradise for me if I could suffer with God, and the greatest pleasures would be hell, were I to enjoy them without him. All my consolation would be to suffer something for him.

I am close to the point of going to see God; I mean to go render him an account. For if I could see God for even one moment, the torments of purgatory would be sweet for me were they to last until the end of the world. What consoles me in this life is that I see God by faith. And I see him in such a way that I can sometimes say, "I no longer believe, I see, for I experience what faith teaches." With this assurance, and by this practice of faith, I will live and die with him.

Always hold fast to God who is the only comfort in your sufferings. I will pray to him to keep you company. My regards to Reverend Mother Prioress. I commend myself to her holy prayers, to the community's, to yours, and I am, in Our Lord,

Yours,

November 17, 1690

NOTES

1. This is the fifth letter with the salutation "Reverend and Dear Mother" (L 3, 4, 5, and 7). We learn that this nun, old and probably an ex-prioress, has a "Mother Prioress" (and not an abbess or superior). This suggests that he may be dealing with the same person in these five letters, and more specifically the Carmelite nun referred to in EL 28.

2. Cf. the Introductory Note to the Letters, pp. 47–48.

3. A pardon and eternal salvation anticipated in faith and trust—both great in Lawrence's case, whose love finds the "sufferings" of the present "agreeable." "My entire consolation would be to suffer something for him," he says further on. He already "sees" God. This is not servile fear, approaching despair.

LETTER 12

To a Nun

[no date]

Reverend Mother,[1]

I will share with you the method I have used to arrive at this state of awareness of God's presence that Our Lord in his mercy has granted me, since you insist that I do so. I cannot hide the repugnance I feel in yielding to your request, even under the condition that you show my letter to no one. If I thought you would let someone see it, all the desire I have for your perfection could not make me comply. This is what I can tell you about it.

In several books I found different methods to approach God and various practices of the spiritual life that I feared would burden my mind rather than facilitate what I wanted and what I sought, namely, a means of being completely disposed to God. This led me to resolve to give all for all. Thus, after offering myself entirely to God in atonement for my sins, I renounced for the sake of his love everything other than God, and I began to live as if only he and I existed in the world.[2] Sometimes I considered myself before him as a miserable criminal at his judge's feet,[3] and at other times I regarded him in my heart as my Father, as my God. I adored him there as often as I could, keeping my mind in his holy presence, and recalling him as many times as I was distracted. I had some trouble doing this exercise, but continued in spite of all the difficulties I encountered, without getting disturbed or anxious when I was involuntarily distracted. I was as faithful to this practice during my activities as I was during my periods of mental prayer, for at every moment, all the time, in the most intense periods of my work I banished and rid from my mind everything that was capable of taking the thought of God away from me.

This, Reverend Mother, is the devotion I have practiced since I entered religious life. Although I have practiced it feebly and imperfectly, I have nonetheless received many advantages from it. I certainly know this is due to the Lord's mercy and goodness—and this must be acknowledged—since we can do nothing without him, myself even less than others. But when we faithfully keep ourselves in his holy presence, seeing him always before us, not only avoiding offending or displeasing him—at least deliberately—but considering him in this fashion, we take the liberty to ask him for the graces we need. So, by repeating these acts they become more familiar, and the practice of the presence of God becomes more natural. Join me in thanking him, please, for his great goodness to me, for I cannot esteem highly enough the great number of graces he bestows on me, a miserable sinner. May he be blessed by all. *Amen.* I am, in our Lord,

Yours,

NOTES

1. If the correspondent had been the same as in L 11, Beaufort would have mentioned it, since these two letters follow each other in sequence. This "Reverend Mother" could have been the "prioress" of L 11 who desired to know more about this good friar of whom the nun of L 11 would have spoken.

2. Lawrence gave himself so radically to God that he attributed every situation and encounter to him.

3. The criminal before the judge; cf. in L 4: "The most miserable one who committed all kinds of crimes" before his King. But in both cases, goodness overwhelms him.

LETTER 13

To a Nun,
A "Daughter of the Blessed Sacrament"

November 28, 1690

Dear Mother,

If we were truly accustomed to the practice of the presence of God, all physical illnesses would be easy to bear. God often permits us to suffer a little in order to purify our souls, and to make us remain with him. I cannot understand how a soul who is with God, and wants him alone, is capable of suffering; I have enough experience of this not to doubt it.

Be courageous. Continually offer him your sufferings while asking him for the strength to bear them. Most of all, get used to conversing with him often, and try never to forget him. Adore him in your infirmities, offer him your sufferings from time to time, even in the midst of your greatest pain. Ask him humbly and lovingly, as a child does his kind father, to be conformed to his holy will, and for the help of his grace. I will help you with my poor, insignificant prayers.

God has various ways to draw us to himself. He sometimes hides from us, but faith alone—never lacking when needed—must be our support and the foundation of our trust, which must be placed entirely in God.

I do not know what God wants to do with me. I am always more content. Everyone is suffering, and I, who should do rigorous penances, experience such continual, profound joys that I have trouble keeping them under control.

I would gladly ask God to share your sufferings, if I did not know the extent of my weakness, which is so great that if he left me alone for a moment I would be the most miserable of creatures. I don't know how he could leave me alone, since faith lets me touch him, and he never withdraws from us unless we first withdraw from him. Let us take care to remain near him. Be with him always. Let us live and die with him. Pray to him for me and for yourself,

    Yours,

NOTE

1. See note 2 of the Introductory Note to the Letters, p 48. The sick nun had exhausted all remedies and treatments (cf. L 14). Lawrence advised surrender and generosity in her sufferings.

LETTER 14

To the Same Nun

[December 21, 1690][1]

Dear Mother,

It hurts me to see you suffer for such a long time. What eases my compassion for your pain is that I know it is the sign of God's love for you; look at it in this way, and you will find it easy to bear. I think you should give up all human remedies and abandon yourself completely to divine providence; perhaps God is only waiting for this abandonment and for a perfect trust in him to cure you. Since these remedies have not had the expected effect in spite of all your efforts—on the contrary, the suffering has increased—resist him no longer, abandon yourself into his hands, and depend entirely on him.

I already told you in my last letter that he sometimes permits physical suffering to cure the illnesses of our souls.[2] Be courageous; make a virtue of necessity. Do not ask God to deliver you from physical suffering, but for the strength to endure courageously for the sake of his love all that he desires, and for as long as he likes.

These prayers, truly somewhat difficult for human nature, please God greatly and comfort those who love him. Love lightens suffering, and when we love God we suffer for him joyfully and courageously; accept it, I beg you. Find consolation in him who is the one and only remedy for all our troubles. He is the father of the afflicted, always ready to come to our aid. He loves us infinitely more than we think. Love him, then. Seek no comfort except in him. I hope you will soon receive it. Goodbye. I will help with my prayers, poor as they are, and will always be, in Our Lord,

Yours,

[P.S.] This morning, the feast of St. Thomas, I received Holy Communion for your intentions.[3]

NOTES

1. "This morning, the feast of St. Thomas," i.e., Thomas the Apostle, December 21. This letter, which presupposes the preceding one (cf. note 2) cannot be from March 7, the feast of St. Thomas Aquinas, which would have occurred after Lawrence's death.

2. Cf. L 13.

3. It was not the custom to receive Holy Communion every day. The *Constitutions* (I, 7, 1–3) permitted communion on Sundays and Thursdays (if there were no other liturgical feasts during the week), as well as feasts such as those of the apostles.

LETTER 15

To the Same Nun

January 22, 1691

Dear Mother,

I thank the Lord for relieving your pain as you desired. I have been ready to die many times,[1] although I had never been so content. Therefore I did not ask for relief but for the strength to suffer courageously, humbly, and lovingly. Courage, dear Mother! Ah, how sweet it is to suffer with God! No matter how great the pain is, accept it with love, for suffering is a paradise as long as we are with him. If we want to enjoy the peace of paradise in this life, we must become accustomed to conversing with him in a familiar, humble and loving manner.

We must restrain our minds from wandering away for any reason whatsoever. We must make our hearts a spiritual temple where we continually adore him. We must keep constant guard over ourselves, not to do, say, or think anything that might displease him. When we are attentive to God in this way, suffering will no longer be anything but sweetness, balm, and consolation.

I know that, to reach this state, the first steps are very difficult, and that we must act purely in faith. Furthermore, we know we can do anything with God's grace,[2] and he never refuses it to those who earnestly ask him for it. Knock at his door, keep knocking, and I tell you that he will open to you in his time[3] if you do not give up, and that he will give you, all at once, what he held off giving for years. Goodbye, pray for me as I do for you. I hope to see him soon. In our Lord,

January 22, 1691

NOTES

1. During his second serious illness; cf. EL 50–51.
2. Cf. Phil 4:13.
3. Cf. Lk 11:8–10.

LETTER 16

To the Same Nun

February 6, 1691

Dear Mother,

God indeed knows what we need, and everything he does is for our good. If we knew how much he loves us, we would readily accept the bitter with the sweet, and even the most painful and difficult things would be pleasant and agreeable. The most painful sufferings do not ordinarily seem unbearable unless we look at them from the wrong perspective. Furthermore, when we are convinced that it is the hand of God at work in us—that he is a Father full of love who allows us to endure humiliation, pain, and suffering—all the bitterness is taken away, and only the sweetness remains.

Let us devote ourselves entirely to knowing God. The more we know him, the more we want to know him. Since love is generally measured by knowledge, the deeper and more extensive the knowledge, the greater will be the love. And if our love is great, we will love him equally in pain and consolation.

Let us not settle for seeking or loving God only for the graces he has given or can give us, no matter how great they may be. These favors, impressive as they are, never bring us as close to him as does a simple act of faith; let us seek him often through this virtue. He is in our midst[1]; let us not look for him elsewhere. Aren't we rude, and even guilty of leaving him alone, when we are occupied with so many trifles that displease and perhaps offend him? He may put up with them, but we should be fearful that they may cost us a great deal some day.

Let us commit ourselves entirely to him, and banish everything else from our hearts and minds. He wants to be alone there, so we should ask him for this grace. If we do what we can, we will soon see the change we hope for in ourselves. I cannot thank him enough for the relief he has given you. I hope for the merciful grace of seeing him in a few days.[2] Let us pray for each other. I am, in Our Lord,

    Yours,

NOTES

1. Cf. Lk 17:21.
2. Brother Lawrence died on February 12, 1691.

IV

CONVERSATIONS

Introductory Note
to the Conversations

Beginning August 3, 1666, Joseph de Beaufort, a young Parisian ecclesiastic, would often visit the old soldier from Lorraine, former cook and now the monastery sandalmaker, who knew much more about the practice of the spiritual life than the learned clerics. From the first visit Beaufort approached Lawrence as if he were a *starets*.[1] Beaufort's account of the first four conversations, spread out between August 3, 1666 and November 25, 1667, has been preserved. Recall the promise Beaufort made in 1693: "Brother Lawrence will speak for himself; I will give you his own words taken from the conversations I had with him, which I wrote down as soon as I had left him" (M 2).

It is not presumptuous to suppose two redactions. First of all, Beaufort rapidly jotted down his notes on paper at the end of a conversation, and then a more serious, better ordered revision was done, perhaps much later, and maybe not even until the time of publication.

Furthermore, there are traces of this more structured editorial work. The text begins with these words, "I saw Brother Lawrence for the first time" (CN 1), which appear to presume the succeeding conversations. And in the fourth conversation, Beaufort speaks of Lawrence's way of approaching God, "which I have already noted" (CN 42). This is less the style of someone taking notes rapidly on the spur of the moment than of an editor who takes into consideration the work as a whole. Lastly and above all, the fact that the four conversations give evidence of few repetitions—rather astounding for conversations separated by large intervals of time—suggests a certain restructuring of the whole work by the editor, who wanted the content to be more varied, more organically presented than it would have been in a conversation that flowed haphazardly with less than perfect sentences.[2] We find ourselves before a Lawrence-Beaufort composite, in which the theme of the conversations is indeed retained, as well as Lawrence's language, "in his own words."

These conclusions are corroborated by the problem of the first pages of the *Spiritual Maxims,* taken from the fourth conversation and developed by Beaufort.[3]

One question remains: Why didn't Beaufort publish these conversations in his first book, dated 1692? It would have been richer without becoming too large. Two answers are possible. Either Beaufort consciously limited the material with a view toward publishing two books,[4] or else, while composing the first book in 1692, Msgr. de Noailles' vicar general, most likely burdened with papers and overworked, could not find his first notes, except one separate sheet, the last from the fourth conversation of 1667, which served as a basis for the elaboration of the first pages of the *Maxims.*

If the texts from the very hand of Brother Lawrence—the greatest part of the *Maxims* and *Letters*—claim priority over our attention, the reader will nonetheless be pleased with these accounts, in which a true mystic is presented by a sincere biographer, rightfully filled with respect and the desire to know the secret of this humble lay brother, whose experience continued to blossom from 1666 to 1667 in remarkable fidelity to the key ideas glimpsed and to the graces received.

NOTES

1. [Russian term for a spiritual father or master.]

2. Another indication of an editorial change: Although Brother Lawrence was 56 years old in 1666, CN 1 states that "forty years" had passed since he had received the special grace at the age of 18. It seems that Beaufort, misinterpreting Brother Lawrence's age, clarifies his account; this might have meant that the effects of this grace were still operative.

3. See the Introductory Note to the *Maxims,* pp. 31–33.

4. This hypothesis seems less plausible because it is less reasonable. In fact, the two works are addressed to the same public and are on the same editorial level.

Conversations

FIRST CONVERSATION

AUGUST 3, 1666

1. I saw Brother Lawrence for the first time, and he told me that God had granted him a special grace of conversion at the age of eighteen when he was still in the world. One day in winter while he was looking at a tree stripped of its leaves, and he realized that in a little while its leaves would reappear, followed by its flowers and fruit, he received a profound insight into God's providence that has never been erased from his soul. This insight completely freed him from the world, and gave him such a love for God that he could not say it had increased during the more than forty years that had passed.[1]

2. He had been the valet of Monsieur de Fieubet, the treasurer of the Savings Bank,[2] and was a clumsy oaf who broke everything.

3. He had asked to be admitted to religious life, thinking he would be skinned alive for his awkwardness and imperfections, and thereby would offer God his life and all its pleasures. But God had fooled him, for he experienced only satisfaction. This led him to tell God frequently: "You have tricked me."

4. [He said] that we must establish ourselves in God's presence by continually conversing with him, and that it was shameful to give up conversation with him to turn to foolishness. We must nourish our souls with an exalted idea of God, and thereby we will draw great joy from being with him. We must enliven our faith, for it is a shame that we have so little. Instead of taking faith as our rule and guide,

we amuse ourselves with insignificant, constantly changing devotions! This way of faith is the mind of the church, and is all we need to reach perfection.

5. We must give ourselves to God entirely and in complete abandonment in the temporal and spiritual realms, finding joy in carrying out his will whether he leads us by the way of suffering or consolation, for it is all the same to one who is completely abandoned. We must remain faithful even in times of aridity when God is testing our love for him. This is when we make suitable acts of resignation and abandonment, a single one of which will result in great progress.

6. [He recounted] how he was not astonished on hearing every day about miseries and sins; on the contrary, he was surprised there were not more, considering the evil of which the sinner is capable. He did pray for sinners, but knowing that God could set them straight when he wanted, he worried no more about it.

7. [He said] that in order to arrive at self-abandonment to God to the extent that he willed, we must watch over all the movements of the soul, since it can become entangled in spiritual things as well as in the most base. God gives the necessary light to those who have the true desire to be with him, and that if I had this intention I could ask to see him whenever I wanted without fear of bothering him, and if not, I ought not come to see him at all.

SECOND CONVERSATION

SEPTEMBER 28, 1666

8. [He said] that he had always been governed by love with no other interest, never worrying whether he would be damned or saved, and having once decided to perform all his actions for the love of God, he was at peace. He was content even when picking up a straw from the ground for the love of God, seeking him alone and nothing else, not even his gifts.

9. [He said] that such behavior of the soul makes God bestow infinite graces upon him. Though we may take the fruit of these graces—that is, the love born from them—we must reject the taste, which is not God, since we know by faith that God is infinitely greater and completely other than what we feel. This manner of acting leads to a marvelous struggle between God and the soul: God gives, and the soul denies that what it receives is God. In this struggle the soul is as strong in faith, or even stronger, than God, since he can never give so much that the soul cannot still deny that the gift is God himself.[3]

10. [He said] that only the soul that trifles with the gift, instead of rejecting it and going beyond it to God, experiences ecstasy and rapture. Except for wonder, we should not allow ourselves to be carried away! God must always remain the master....

11. [Brother Lawrence said] that God rewards everything we do for him so promptly and so generously that he sometimes wished he could hide from him what he was doing for God's love so that, by renouncing all reward, he would have the pleasure of doing something purely for God!

12. He had been greatly troubled in spirit, thinking that he was surely damned, and no one in the world could have convinced him otherwise! But he reasoned in this way: "I entered religious life solely for the love of God and have tried to act for him alone. Whether I be damned or saved, I always want to act purely for his love; at least I can say that, until I die, I will do whatever I can to love him...." This anxiety lasted four very painful years.[4] Since that time he thought about neither heaven nor hell. His whole life was nothing but freedom[5] and continual joy! He placed his sins between God and himself, as if to tell God that he did not deserve his graces, but that did not stop God from filling him with them! God sometimes took him by the hand and brought him before the whole heavenly court, showing off this miserable sinner whom he was pleased to shower with his graces.

13. [He said] that in the beginning we must work at forming the habit of continually conversing with God, attributing to him everything we do; but after a little effort we will feel ourselves awakened by love with no more difficulty.

14. He expected that, after the good times God had given him, he would have his share of suffering and pain. He did not worry about it, however, knowing well that since he could do nothing by himself, God would not hesitate to give him the strength necessary to bear them.

15. When faced with some virtue to be practiced he would say, "My God, I can only do this if you help me," and he received the necessary strength immediately, and even more.

16. When he failed he did nothing other than acknowledge his failure, telling God, "I will never do anything right if you leave me alone; it's up to you to stop me from falling and correct what is wrong." After that he no longer worried about his failure.

17. [He said] that we must act very straightforwardly with God, and speak to him freely, asking him for help in events as they happen, for God never fails to come to our aid, as he often experienced. He had recently been asked to go to Burgundy to get the wine supply, a painful task for him. Not only did he lack skill in these matters, but his leg was crippled and he could only get about on the boat by dragging himself over the barrels. Yet he did not worry about it or about his purchase of wine! He told God it was his problem, after

which he discovered that all was accomplished, and all was done well! He had been sent to Auvergne[6] the previous year for the same reason. He could not explain how the matter was accomplished since he was not the one who accomplished it, and yet it was done well.

18. The same was true of the kitchen to which he had the strongest natural aversion. He got used to doing everything for the love of God, asking him at every opportunity for the grace to do his work. He was able to carry it out with great ease for the fifteen years he was in charge of it.[7]

19. He was assigned to the sandal shop, which was a delight for him, but he was willing to give up this task like the others. He would find joy everywhere doing little things for the love of God.

20. [He said] that the periods of mental prayer were not at all different for him than other times. He made his retreats when Father Prior told him to do so, but he neither desired them nor asked for them, since his most demanding work in no way turned him away from God.

21. Knowing that we must love God in all things and striving to fulfill this obligation, he had no need of a director,[8] but a great need for a confessor to receive absolution for the sins he committed. He acknowledged his sins and was not surprised by them. He confessed them to God and did not plead before him to excuse them; after that he returned to his ordinary exercises of love and adoration in peace.

22. [He said] that he consulted no one in his troubles. With the light of faith and the knowledge that God was present, he was satisfied to act for him come what may, and he was willing to lose himself for the love of God, and he was indeed content.

23. [He said] that thoughts[9] spoil everything; that's how trouble starts! We must be careful to reject them as soon as we notice that they have nothing to do with our present occupation or our salvation, and begin again our conversation with God, which is where our good is found.

24. In the beginning he had often spent the whole period of mental prayer fighting off thoughts and falling into them again. He was never able to pray by rules like others; he would meditate [discursively] for a while in the beginning but afterward he did not know how it went, and it would be impossible for him to explain it.

25. He asked to remain a novice forever, not believing that anyone would want to receive his profession and unable to imagine that these two years had passed....

26. [He said] that he was not bold enough to ask God for penances, that he really didn't want to do any, but he knew well that he deserved many, and that when God would send them to him, he would give him the grace to do them. All penances and other exercises serve only as a means to reach union with God by love. Once he had considered this carefully, he realized it was shorter to go straight there by an exercise of continual love, by doing everything for the love of God!

27. [He said] that the actions of the understanding are very different from those of the will, for the former amounted to little, while the latter were everything. Only loving and rejoicing with God truly matter.

28. Even if we did all the penances possible, they would not so much as take away one single sin if they were separated from love! Without worrying, we must look to the blood of Christ for the remission of sin, working only at loving God with our whole heart. God seems to choose the worst sinners to give the greatest graces, rather than those who remain innocent, because that shows his goodness more.

29. [He said] that he thought neither of death, nor of his sins, nor of paradise, nor of hell, but only of doing little things for the love of God, since he was not capable of doing great things. Other than that, whatever happened to him was God's will, and he was at peace with it.

30. [He said] that even when someone offended him deeply, it was nothing when compared with the inner suffering he had endured or the profound joys he had often experienced. Since nothing worried him or frightened him, he would ask God only that he be preserved from offending him.

31. He told me that he was rarely scrupulous. "When I realize I have failed, I acknowledge it and say: this is typical; it's all I can do! If I have succeeded, I thank God and acknowledge that this grace comes from him."

THIRD CONVERSATION

NOVEMBER 22, 1666

32. He told me that the foundation of his spiritual life was an exalted idea and esteem of God in faith. Once he conceived it, his only concern was, in the beginning, to faithfully reject every other thought, and to perform all his actions for the love of God. Sometimes a long time would pass without his thinking about God, yet this did not disturb him. After he acknowledged his lowliness to God, he returned to him with a degree of trust equal to the misery he had experienced earlier when he had forgotten him.

33. [He said] that the trust we have in God honors him greatly and brings us great graces. God cannot deceive, nor can he permit a soul, abandoned to himself and resolved to endure everything for him, to suffer for a long time.

34. He reached the point where his thoughts were exclusively of God. In his struggle against temptation, he could sense the temptation from the first moment. His experience of God's prompt help was such, however, that he sometimes allowed the temptations to advance, but at just the right moment he called upon God, and they vanished completely. Similarly, when he had some matter to take care of, he never thought about it in advance, but within the necessary time period he found in God, as in a clear mirror, what he needed at the moment. For some time now he acted in this manner with no apprehension, although before he had this experience of God's prompt help he worried about everything.

35. He remembered none of the things he did, and was hardly even aware of them while he was doing them, so that on getting up from the table he did not know what he had eaten! He acted in simplicity in keeping with his understanding, and thus did everything for the love of God. He gave him thanks for directing his projects and a multitude of other activities. He did everything quite straightforwardly and in such a way that he remained rooted in the loving presence of God.

36. When his duties distracted him somewhat[10] from thinking about God, God impressed a remembrance of himself on his soul, giving him so intense an awareness of God, warming and inflaming him so strongly, that he cried out and made exaggerated gestures, singing and jumping about like a fool.[11]

37. He was more closely united with God during his ordinary activities than when he put them aside to do his retreat exercises, which generally left him in great aridity.

38. [He said] that he expected great physical or mental suffering to occur, and that his greatest trial would be to lose the perceptible[12] awareness of God he had experienced for so long. But God's goodness assured him he would never abandon him, and would give him the strength to endure whatever evil he would permit to happen to him. With that assurance he feared nothing, nor had he any need to communicate with anyone concerning the state of his soul. Whenever he had tried to do that, he came out of it feeling more perplexed. In wanting to die and lose himself for the love of God, he feared nothing, for total surrender to God is the sure way, along which there is always light to guide us.

39. In the beginning we must faithfully act and renounce ourselves, and after that come only unspeakable delights. In times of difficulty we have no recourse but to Jesus Christ, to ask him for his grace that makes everything easy.

40. We settle for penances and private devotions, leaving aside love, our end. Our works prove this, and that is why we see so little solid virtue.

41. Neither finesse nor learning is required to approach God, only a heart resolved to devote itself exclusively to him, and to love him alone.

FOURTH CONVERSATION

NOVEMBER 25, 1667

42. Brother Lawrence spoke to me with great fervor and openness of his way of approaching God, as I have in part already noted. He told me that what matters is renouncing once and for all everything that we recognize does not lead to God, in order to become accustomed to a continual conversation with him, without mystery or finesse. We need only to recognize him present within us, to speak with him at every moment, and to ask for his help, so that we will know his will in perplexing events, and will be able to carry out those things we clearly see he asks of us, offering them to him before doing them, and thanking him afterward for completing them. During this continual conversation we are thus taken up in praising, adoring, and ceaselessly loving God for his infinite goodness and perfection.

43. We must ask him for his grace with full confidence, paying no attention to our thoughts, relying on the infinite merits of Our Lord. God, at every opportunity, always bestows his grace. Brother Lawrence saw this clearly and lacked this awareness only when he was distracted from God's company, or if he had forgotten to ask him for his help. In times of doubt God always gives light so long as our only concern is to please him and to act for the sake of his love.

44. [He said] that our sanctification depends not on changing our works, but on doing for God what we would normally do for ourselves. It is a pity to see how many people are attached to certain

97

works that they perform rather imperfectly and for human respect, always mistaking the means for the end.

45. He found no better way to approach God than by the ordinary works required in his case by obedience, purifying them as much as he could from all human respect, and doing them for the pure love of God.

46. [He said] that it is a big mistake to think that the period of mental prayer should be different from any other. We must be just as closely united with God during our activities as we are during our times of prayer.

47. [He said] that, for him, mental prayer had become the experience of God's presence, his soul having withdrawn from everything except love. He hardly noticed any difference outside of this time since he kept himself close to God, praising and blessing him with all his strength, spending his life in continual joy, yet hoping that God would give him something to suffer when he was stronger.

48. [He said] that we must entrust ourselves to God and to him alone, once and for all, and he will not deceive us.

49. We must never tire of doing little things for the love of God who considers not the magnitude of the work, but the love.[13] In the beginning we must not be surprised if we often fail; in the end, once the habit is formed, we will able to act without thinking about it and with great delight.

50. We must cultivate faith, hope, and love, for these alone can conform us completely to the will of God. All other things are insignificant and we must not settle for them, but rather regard them as a bridge to be crossed quickly so we can lose ourselves in our sole end by confidence and love.

51. Everything is possible for one who believes, still more for one who hopes, [even more for one who loves,][14] and most of all for one who practices and perseveres in these three virtues.

52. Our goal is to be the most perfect adorers of God in this life, as we hope to be throughout all eternity.

53. When we undertake the spiritual life we must seriously consider who we are, recognizing that we are worthy of all scorn, unworthy of the name Christian, and subject to all kinds of miseries and a multitude of setbacks. These disturb us and make our health, our moods, our inner dispositions and their outward manifestations

changeable; in all, we are persons God wants to humble by means of a multitude of internal and external troubles and trials. We must believe that it is advantageous for us and pleasing to God to sacrifice ourselves to him; that it is normal for his divine providence to abandon us to all sorts of trials, miseries and temptations. Once we recognize this, should we be surprised that we experience suffering, temptation, opposition, and contradiction from our neighbor? On the contrary, we must submit to these things and bear them as long as God so wills, just as we would those things we find beneficial.

54. A soul depends on grace in proportion to its desire for greater perfection.

NOTES

1. See the Introductory Note to the *Conversations,* p. 88, note 2. It would have been more accurate to say "more than 34 years."

2. Gaspard de Fieubet (1577–1647), treasurer of the Savings Bank, husband of Claude Ardier, father of four children; see *Dictionnaire de biographie française* (Paris: Letouzey et Ané, 1975), vol. 13, col. 1311–1312.

3. The theme of "negative theology" is evident here.

4. There was, therefore, "during the first ten years" in the monastery where he "suffered greatly" (L 2), a recurrence of emotional turmoil during the years 1647–1650. See our work *Vie et Pensées du frère Laurent,* where we consider in greater depth Brother Lawrence's spiritual journey.

5. "Freedom," here in the sense of a great inner freedom.

6. Regarding the trips to Bourgogne (1666) and Auvergne (1665) see the General Introduction p. xx.

7. See EL 33, note 22.

8. Even though Lawrence said that he "consulted no one regarding his sufferings" (CN 22), he did nonetheless open himself to a spiritual director (see L 2), though often to no benefit (CN 23).

9. "Thoughts," in the sense of withdrawing into his own reflections, and different from "our conversation with God" (CN 23). Lawrence found no satisfaction in discursive reasoning, which, nonetheless, he practiced in the beginning of his Carmelite life (cf. CN 24 and L 2).

10. In CN 32, it is a question of going "sometimes a long time" without thinking of God.

11. Cf. L 1, note 4.

12. "Perceptibly" here cannot refer to superficial sentiments: Lawrence recommends holy indifference vis-a-vis "consolations" (cf. CN 5), the preference for God "alone" and "not his gifts" (CN 8), for God is "beyond his gifts" (CN 10). The "feeling" here is the reality of union with God, which Lawrence has been experiencing "for so long" (CN 38).

13. Cf. St. Teresa of Avila, *Castle* 7, 4, 15: "The Lord doesn't look so much at the greatness of our works as at the love with which they are done."

14. In keeping with SM 1 and the logic of the text, we have completed the passage.

V

THE PRACTICE
OF THE
PRESENCE OF GOD

Introductory Note
to the Practice of the Presence of God

If our hypothesis is correct, Beaufort would have found his notes for the *Conversations* [1] after some time had passed. This enables us to better understand the immediate goal of the *Practice*, as well as the *Ways*—the other biographical sketch to be dealt with shortly—namely, to fill out the second book on Brother Lawrence that otherwise would have been rather meager. Whatever the case may be, the second book of 1694 gives, in about twelve pages, the *Practice of the presence of God, taken from the Writings of Brother Lawrence,* an anthology of fine texts derived from the *Letters* and also from the *Maxims,* as can be seen from our notes. There is nothing new here, therefore, simply a summary of Brother Lawrence's doctrine; a text, furthermore, that seems to have pleased his readers. For that reason we have decided to include it in this edition. Our notes will be limited to identifying the original document from which a particular passage, indicated by quotation marks, is taken. [2]

NOTES

1. See the Introductory Note to the *Conversations,* p. 88.
2. In the third edition of 1710, the publisher (Pierre Poiret, most likely) did not realize that *all* the texts of the *Practice* constituted borrowings. This is why he added, unnecessarily, the texts he did not find in the *Maxims,* thus supporting a specious hypothesis concerning two editors who would have drawn from the same source manuscripts (see *La Theologie de la presence de Dieu,* "Avis de l'imprimeur," p. 3–4).

Practice of the
Presence of God

"The holiest and most necessary practice in the spiritual life is that of the presence of God. It consists in taking delight in and becoming accustomed to his divine company, speaking humbly and conversing lovingly with him all the time, at every moment, without rule or measure; especially in times of temptation, suffering, aridity, weariness, even infidelity and sin" [cf. SM 6].

"We must continually apply ourselves so that all our actions become a kind of brief conversation with God, not in a contrived manner, but coming from the purity and simplicity of our hearts" [cf. SM 7].

"We must perform all our actions carefully and deliberately, not impulsively or hurriedly, for such would characterize a distracted mind. We must work gently and lovingly with God, asking him to accept our work, and by this continual attention to God we will crush the head of the devil and force the weapons from his hands" [cf. SM 8].

"During our work and other activities, even during our reading, no matter how spiritual, and even during our religious exercises and vocal prayers, we must stop for a moment, as often as possible, to adore God in the depths of our hearts, to savor him even though in passing and on the sly, to praise him, to ask his help, to offer him our hearts, and to thank him. Nothing is more pleasing to God than [for us] to turn away from all creatures many times throughout the day to withdraw and adore him present within. We can offer God no greater evidence of our fidelity than by frequently renouncing

and scorning creatures in order to enjoy their Creator for a moment. This exercise gradually destroys the self-love only found
among creatures. Turning to God frequently rids us of self-love without our even realizing it" [cf. SM 9].

"This presence of God is the soul's life and nourishment,
which can be acquired by the Lord's grace. Here are the means: a
great purity of life" [cf. SM 26-27], "keeping constant guard not to
do, say, or think anything that might displease God" [cf. L 15]; and
when something like that happens, to humbly ask him pardon and
do penance for it[1]; "a great fidelity to the practice of this presence
and to the fostering of this awareness of God within, which must
always be carried out gently, humbly, and lovingly, without giving in
to any disturbance" [cf. SM 28].

"We must take special care that this inner awareness precedes
our activities somewhat, that it accompanies them from time to
time, and that we complete all of them in the same way. We must
not get discouraged when we forget this holy practice," for all that is
needed is to calmly take it up again; "once the habit is formed we
will find contentment in everything" [cf. SM 29].

In order "to arrive at this state, mortification of the senses is
presupposed, since it is impossible for a soul that still finds some satisfaction in creatures to completely enjoy this divine presence; for
to be with God, we must abandon creatures" [cf. SM 32].

"God desires to possess our heart completely; if we do not
empty it of everything other than himself, he cannot act nor do
there what he pleases" [cf. L 3]. "He often complains of our blindness, and cries out ceaselessly that we deserve sympathy for settling
for so little. 'I have,' he says, 'infinite treasures to give you, yet you
are satisfied with a bit of perceptible devotion that passes in an instant.' In this way we bind God's hands and halt the abundant flow
of his graces" [cf. L 1].

To advance in "the practice of the presence of God we should
let go of all our cares, including a multitude of private devotions,
good in themselves but often carried out for the wrong reason, for
these devotions are nothing more than the means to arrive at the
end. If, then, we are with the one who is our end by this practice of
the presence of God, it is useless to return to the means. We can

continue our loving exchange with him, remaining in his holy presence, sometimes by an act of adoration, other times by acts of oblation, thanksgiving, or anything else our minds can devise" [cf. L 4].

"We do not always have to be in church to be with God. We can make of our hearts an oratory where we can withdraw from time to time to converse with him there. Everyone is capable of these familiar conversations with God" [cf. L 9]. " 'A brief lifting up of the heart is enough,' writes Brother Lawrence, recommending this practice to a gentleman, 'a brief remembrance of God, an act of inner adoration, even though on the run with sword in hand. These prayers, short as they may be, are very pleasing to God, and far from leaving us fearful, strengthen us in the most dangerous of circumstances. Keep this in mind as often as possible; this manner of prayer is very necessary for a soldier always exposed to threats to his life and often to his salvation'" [cf. L 6].

This practice of the presence of God is very helpful for "mental prayer, for it will be easier to remain calm during mental prayer when the mind, not allowed to take flight during the day, is kept faithfully in God's presence" [cf. L 7].

Since "all of life is full of dangers and hazards, it is impossible to avoid them without God's constant help. We cannot ask him for it if we are not with him. We cannot be with him unless we think of him often. We cannot think of him often except by a holy habit" [cf. L 8] of keeping ourselves in his presence, "asking him for the graces we need at every moment" [cf. L 12].

Nothing can comfort us more in life's trials and sufferings than this intimate conversation with God.[2] Practiced faithfully, "all physical illnesses will be easy to bear. God often permits us to suffer in order to purify our souls and to make us remain with him. If we are with God, and want him alone, we are incapable of suffering. We must therefore adore him in our infirmities, offering him our sufferings from time to time, asking him lovingly, as a child does his father, to be conformed to his holy will, and for the help of his grace" [cf. L 13]. These short prayers are very appropriate for the sick and are an excellent remedy for pain.[3]

"Suffering is paradise as long as we are with God. This means we must become accustomed to conversing with God even when we are suffering, and restrain our minds from wandering away from him. When we are sick we must keep constant guard over ourselves not to do, say, or think anything, in an attempt to ease the pain, that might displease him. When we are attentive to God in this way, suffering will no longer be anything but sweetness, balm and consolation" [cf. L 15].

"The worldly do not understand these truths, and I am not surprised, because illnesses are considered as natural afflictions and not as graces from God. Those who regard them as coming from the hand of God, as signs of his mercy and the means he uses for their salvation, ordinarily find great consolation in them" [cf. L 11].

NOTES

1. Sentence from Beaufort, perhaps evoking CN 15–16 or L 7.
2. Sentence from Beaufort, evoking passages from L 11, 13, 14, 15, 16.
3. Sentence from Beaufort, evoking passages from L 11, 13, 14, 15, 16.

VI

THE WAYS
OF BROTHER LAWRENCE

Introductory Note to the Ways

Here, originally intended for the second book on Brother Lawrence, is a new presentation of the spiritual profile and main biographical data of the lay brother. Joseph de Beaufort speaks as an eyewitness: "I will write what I myself heard and saw concerning the ways of Brother Lawrence" (W 1). He carefully avoids repeating what is already presented in the *Eulogy*, except for the narration of Lawrence's last illness and death, copied more or less literally from EL 55–60.

The author relies on the *Conversations,* for the most part, to propose to us Lawrence's "virtues" (W 2) and present him as an "excellent model of solid piety" (W 1)—the principal purpose of the *Ways*—and analysis will reveal just how much he drew from them, even verbally. He will have recourse only once to the *Letters,* that is, to the texts from Lawrence himself. That leads us to think that Beaufort, when he quotes Lawrence, attaches more importance to the spirit and totality of the words and expressions heard repeatedly than to the exact formulation at a particular moment. We have a comparable example in the *Eulogy* (EL 28).

Beaufort will elaborate on fidelity to the faith of the church, the "living interpreter" of the Gospel (W 22–24) and on Lawrence as the "wise Christian""(W 30), citing mainly Clement of Alexandria and Gregory Nazianzen (W 30–31). He concludes with Lawrence's relevance for both religious and laity.

Ways
of Brother Lawrence

1. I will write what I myself have heard and seen concerning the ways of Brother Lawrence, a Discalced Carmelite friar of blessed memory, who died about two years ago at the monastery in Paris.

Someone[1] who chose to occupy the last place in God's house rather than keep his higher rank among sinners, who preferred the disgrace of Christ to the feasts and delights of Egypt,[2] wanted me to inform those souls disillusioned with the love of the present times of what he knew I had gathered from Brother Lawrence's teachings.

I will gladly comply. Even though we have already given the public a *Eulogy* and some *Letters,* I maintain that we cannot overemphasize what we have preserved from this holy man.

I believe it would be helpful to recognize him as an excellent model of solid piety at a time when practically everyone finds virtue where it is not, and takes the wrong paths to get there.[3]

2. Brother Lawrence will speak for himself. I will give you his own words taken from the conversations I had with him, which I wrote down as soon as I left him. No one portrays the saints better than they do themselves. The *Confessions* and the *Letters* of Saint Augustine present a much more natural portrait than anything that could be said about him. Nothing will make this servant of God, whose virtues I will propose to you, better known than what he himself has said in the simplicity of his heart.

3. Brother Lawrence's virtue never made him harsh. His heart was open, eliciting confidence, letting you feel you could tell him anything, and that you had found a friend. For his part, once he

knew who he was dealing with, he spoke freely and showed great goodness. What he said was simple, yet always appropriate, and made good sense. Once you got past his rough exterior you discovered an unusual wisdom, a freedom beyond the reach of the ordinary lay brother, an insight that extended far beyond what you would expect. When he was seeking alms[4] you could see he was suited to conduct the most serious business, and you could consult him on anything. Such was the appearance Brother Lawrence gave.

4. He himself depicted his attitudes and interior life in the conversations I gave you. His conversion began, as I indicated,[5] by an exalted idea he had conceived of the power and wisdom of God, which he carefully fostered by faithfully dispelling every other thought.[6] Since this first awareness of God was in effect the basis of all Brother Lawrence's perfection, it would be appropriate to pause to consider how he developed it.

5. Faith was the only light he used, not only to know God in the beginning, but from that point on; he wanted only to be instructed and led by faith in all God's ways. He told me several times that everything he said, read, and even wrote himself seemed insipid in comparison with what faith revealed to him concerning the grandeurs of God and Jesus Christ. "He alone," he said, "is capable of making himself known as he really is. We seek in reasoning and in the sciences—as in a poor copy—what we fail to see in an excellent original. God paints himself in the depths of our souls, yet we do not want to see him there. We leave him for foolish things and fail to converse with our King, who is always present within us. It is not enough to love God and to know him from what books tell us, or from what we feel in our souls, or from a few insignificant impulses of devotion, or from some insight. We must make our faith come alive and lift ourselves up by means of it beyond all our feelings, to adore God and Jesus Christ in all their divine perfections, as they are in themselves. This way of faith is the mind of the church, and suffices to reach a high degree of perfection."[7]

6. He not only contemplated God present by faith in his soul, but in everything he saw, in everything that happened, he would raise himself up, going from the creature to the Creator. A tree he saw dried up in winter lifted him up immediately to God, and inspired him with so sublime an awareness that this impression was

still as strong and intense in his soul forty years later.[8] Thus at every opportunity he would use visible things to reach the invisible.

7. For the same reason, of the little reading he did, he preferred the holy Gospel to all other books because in it he found pure, simple nourishment for his faith in the very words of Jesus Christ.

8. Brother Lawrence began by faithfully cultivating this exalted awareness of God's presence, contemplated by faith, in his heart. He fostered this awareness by continuous acts of adoration and love, invoking Our Lord's help in what he had to do, and then thanking him after doing it.[9] He asked pardon for his sins, admitting them, as he said, without bargaining with God.[10] Since his occupations were bound up with these acts and provided material for them, he accomplished them with greater ease,[11] and far from distracting him from his work, they helped him do it well.[12]

9. He admitted, however, that there were considerable periods of time when he was not mindful of this practice, but after humbly confessing his fault, he would take it up again without difficulty.[13] Sometimes a host of inappropriate thoughts would violently seize the place of his God, but he was satisfied to put them aside gently and return to his ordinary conversation.[14] Thus his fidelity was rewarded with a continuous awareness of God. His various, multiple acts were changed into a simple view,[15] an enlightened love, an uninterrupted joy.[16]

"The times of activity are not at all different from the hours of prayer,"[17] he said, "for I possess God as peacefully in the commotion of my kitchen, where often enough several people are asking me for different things at the same time, as I do when kneeling before the Blessed Sacrament. My faith sometimes becomes so enlightened I think I've lost it,[18] for it seems to me that the curtain of obscurity has been drawn aside, and the endless, clear day of the next life has begun to dawn."

This is where his determination to reject[19] all other thoughts in order to devote himself to a continual conversation with God led Brother Lawrence. Eventually it became so familiar that he said it had become almost impossible for him to turn away[20] from God to deal with anything else.

10. You will find an important remark on this subject in his conversations, where he said that this presence of God must be maintained more by the heart and by love than by the understanding or by discourse. "In the ways of God," he said, "thoughts amount to little whereas love counts for everything.[21] And it is not necessary," he continued, "to have important things to do."[22] I am describing a lay brother in the kitchen to you, so let me use his own expressions: "I flip my little omelette in the frying pan for the love of God, and when it's done, if I have nothing to do, I prostrate myself on the floor and adore my God who gave me the grace to do it, after which I get up happier than a king. When I can do nothing else, it is enough for me to pick up a straw from the ground for the love of God."[23]

"We look for methods," he continued, "to learn how to love God. We want to get there by I don't know how many practices. A multitude of methods makes it more difficult for us to remain in God's presence. Isn't it much shorter and more direct to do everything for the love of God,[24] to use all the works of our state in life[25] to manifest our love to him, and to foster the awareness of his presence in us by this exchange of our heart with him? Finesse is not necessary.[26] We need only approach him directly and straightforwardly." I have faithfully kept his typical expressions.

11. We must not conclude, however, that it is enough to love God and offer him our works, to invoke his help and perform acts of love. Brother Lawrence did not attain the perfection of love by these means alone, but because he was most careful from the very beginning to do nothing that might displease God.[27] He had renounced everything but God,[28] and he had forgotten himself completely.

"Since I entered religious life," these are his words, "I no longer think about virtue or my salvation.[29] After giving myself entirely to God in atonement for my sins, and after renouncing everything for his love,[30] I believed my only task for the rest of my days was to live as if only God and I existed in the world."[31]

This is how Brother Lawrence began, by the more perfect way, thus leaving everything for God and doing everything for love of him. He forgot himself entirely. He no longer thought about heaven or hell, nor about his past or present sins,[32] once he asked pardon of God. He never went back over his confessions,[33] for he entered a state of perfect peace once he had confessed his sins to God,[34] and that was all he could do.[35] After that he "abandoned himself to God," as he said, "for life or death, for time and eternity."

12. "We are made for God alone," he would say, "who can only be pleased when we turn away from ourselves to devote ourselves to him. In him we clearly see what we ourselves lack, yet even our reflecting on what we lack may be a remnant of self-love that, under the appearance of perfection, holds us bound and hinders us from lifting ourselves up to God."

13. Brother Lawrence said he never swayed from his initial determination in spite of the terrible sufferings he had for four years, so terrible that he was certain he was damned and no one could have convinced him otherwise. Without thinking about what would become of him, and without concerning himself with his sufferings (as troubled souls would do) he consoled himself by saying, "Come what may, at least I will do everything for the love of God for the rest of my life." Therefore, by forgetting himself he resolved to lose himself for God, and this worked to his advantage.[36]

14. In him the love of God's will had taken the place of the attachment we ordinarily have to our own. He saw only God's plan in what happened to him, and this kept him in continual peace. When he learned of some evil, instead of being astonished by it, he was, on the contrary, surprised that things were not worse, given the malice of which the sinner is capable. Brother Lawrence would immediately turn to God who, he realized, could remedy the situation,[37] and who permitted these evils for just reasons, beneficial to the general order of his action in the world. Once he prayed for sinners, he no longer worried about them and returned to his state of peace.

15. I said to him one day, without warning, that something of considerable importance, very close to his heart and for which he had worked a long time, could not be carried out and, in fact, the opposite had just been decided. His only reply was: "We must believe that those who made this decision did so for good reasons. Our task is to implement it and not to speak of it any more." That is in fact what he did, and so completely that he never spoke of it again even though he often had the opportunity.

16. A very important man[38] went to see Brother Lawrence, who was seriously ill, and asked him which he would choose: if God permitted, to remain alive longer to increase his merits, or to receive them now in heaven. Without deliberating, Brother Lawrence answered that he would leave the choice to God, and that, as far as he was concerned, he had only to wait peacefully until God revealed his will.

17. This disposition left him with such great indifference to all things and in such complete freedom that it resembled the state of the blessed. He took no sides. You could detect no preference or particular inclination in him. Our natural attachments, even for the holiest places or for one's country,[39] did not concern him. He was equally liked by those who held opposite opinions. He wanted the common good without reference to those for whom or by whom it was brought about. Citizen of heaven, nothing held him bound on earth. His viewpoints were not limited to time. By contemplating the Eternal One for so long he had become eternal like him.

18. He was content with any place, with any task.[40] Brother Lawrence found God everywhere, while repairing sandals or praying with the community.[41] He had no particular desire to go on retreat because he found in his ordinary work the same God to love[42] and adore as can be found in the most remote desert.

19. His sole approach to God was to do everything for his love,[43] and so it made no difference to him what he did,[44] provided that he did it for God. It was God, not the thing itself, that concerned him. He knew that the more opposed to his natural inclination the work was, the more valuable was the love with which he offered it to God. The smallness of the thing in no way diminished the worth of his offering, because God, who needs nothing, considers only the love accompanying our works.[45]

20. Another characteristic of Brother Lawrence was an extraordinary steadfastness that in another walk of life[46] might be called boldness. It revealed a great soul that rose above the fear and hope of everything but God. He admired nothing, nothing surprised him, and he feared nothing. His stability of soul came from the same source as all the other virtues. The exalted idea he conceived of God represented God to him as sovereign justice and infinite good, as he really is. Relying on these virtues, he was convinced

God would not deceive him,[47] and would bring about only what was for his good, since he, for his part, was resolved never to displease God, and to do and suffer everything for his love.

21. I asked him one day who his spiritual director was. He told me he had none and did not think he needed one[48] since the *Rule* and his religious obligations made clear what his duties were, and the Gospel obliged him to love God with his whole heart. Once he realized this a director seemed unnecessary to him, but he greatly needed a confessor to absolve his sins.

22. Those who conduct themselves in the spiritual life only according to their own inclinations and preferences, who think they have nothing more important to do than determine whether or not they have devotion, this type of person cannot be stable or be on the right path because these things continually change,[49] either due to our own negligence or by the order of God who varies his gifts and his action over us according to our needs.

Brother Lawrence, on the contrary, steadfast in the way of unchanging faith, was always even-tempered because all his efforts were directed exclusively to carrying out the duties of the place where God put him, considering only the virtues of his state in life as his reward. Instead of paying attention to his dispositions and examining the road he was walking, he looked only at God, the end of the journey. Therefore he made great strides toward him by practicing justice, charity, and humility, more intent on doing than on thinking about what he was doing.

23. Brother Lawrence's devotion, based as it was on this solid foundation, was not at all subject to visions or other extraordinary revelations. He was convinced that these, even when authentic, most often signified the weakness of a soul that seeks God's gifts rather than God himself.[50] And, except for the time of his novitiate, he experienced nothing of this kind[51]; at least he said nothing about it to those he trusted the most and to whom he opened his heart. Throughout his life he followed in the steps of the saints along the sure way of faith. He never strayed from the ordinary way that leads to salvation by the practices authorized by the church for all time, by good deeds, and the virtues of his state in life. He was suspicious of everything else. His good sense and the light he drew from the simplicity of his faith preserved him from all the hazards present in

the spiritual life that cause so many souls today to end up ship-wrecked,[52] because they give themselves over to the love of novelty, to their own imagination, to curiosity, and to the ways of the world.

24. Avoiding these pitfalls is so easy when we seek God alone. When it comes to religion, everything that seems new must be carefully evaluated. This most necessary virtue is not among those things that improve with the passing of time. On the contrary, our religion was perfect from its origin. Jesus Christ taught his church everything essential, either directly or by the Holy Spirit speaking through the apostles, and we must turn to the church to find our security.

It is true that besides this faith, written down and taught orally, the body of Jesus Christ—present on earth in the faithful—needed a living interpreter to explain his will and to indicate the way we must follow should doubts arise. The Savior provided for this. The church he founded speaks through its body of pastors to whom he gave the authority to propose and explain doctrine, and to prescribe for each of the faithful the way of salvation according to the rule of faith. The faith of the church is the sure way that keeps the soul in complete peace, that fulfills all its desires, and that consoles it fully in its exile.

If that were insufficient and we wanted to go beyond it; if we wanted to abandon the opinions and devotions based on faith for the sake of those merely tolerated by the church in deference to its children's weakness; if, due to anxiety or curiosity, we were to follow the example of an individual who strays from the ordinary way; if, in seeking our own will, we were to prefer our own ideas to the teachings of the church, then we would be deliberately exposing ourselves to danger, and we would have become companions of those who are lost because of a voluntary illusion.

God, having spoken through the Fathers and the Prophets, has at last spoken through his Son[53]; this Son teaches us today through the church. The faith it teaches is sure, complete, and sufficient. Let us hold fast to it. This holy friar followed it perfectly and provides us in his person with an excellent model of the way that leads directly to God.

25. Prepared by his manner of living, and following so sure a way, he calmly faced the approach of death without anxiety. His

patience, so great throughout his life, increased even more when he approached his end. It looked as if he never had a moment's discomfort[54] even when his illness was the most painful. Joy appeared not only on his face but even in his manner of speaking, causing the friars who visited him to ask him if he really was in pain. "Pardon me," he said, "I am in pain. My side hurts but my spirit is at peace." But they added, "if God wanted you to suffer these pains for ten years, would you be willing?" "I would be," he said, "not only for that number of years, but I would gladly consent to endure these sufferings until the Day of Judgment, if God wanted, and I would hope he would give me the grace to always remain so resigned."

26. As the hour for his departure from this world approached, he would often cry out, "O Faith! O Faith!" expressing more about its importance in this way than if he had uttered many words. He adored God continually, and said to one of the friars that he hardly believed in the presence of God in his soul any more, because by means of this luminous faith he already caught a glimpse of this intimate presence.

27. His courage was so great, during a most frightening time, that he said to one of his friends who was questioning him on this subject that he feared neither death, nor hell, nor God's judgment, nor the devil's efforts. Since they were so pleased to hear such edifying statements, they continued to question him. They asked him if he knew it was a terrible thing to fall into the hands of the living God,[55] because no matter who you are, you cannot know for sure if you are worthy of love or hatred.[56] "I agree," he said, "but I would not want to know, for I am afraid of becoming proud; the best thing is to abandon yourself to God."

28. After he received the last sacraments, a friar asked him what he was doing and what was occupying his mind. "I am doing what I will be doing throughout eternity," he replied. "I am blessing God, I am praising God, I am adoring God, and I am loving him with my whole heart. This is what our vocation is all about, brothers, to adore God, and to love him without worrying about anything else."

29. These were Brother Lawrence's last sentiments. He died shortly thereafter in the same peace and tranquility that had characterized his life. He died on February 12, 1691, at about eighty years of age.[57]

30. Nothing gives us a clearer picture of the true Christian philosopher [58] than what was just cited regarding the life and death of this fine friar. Such were those of former days who truly renounced the world to devote themselves exclusively to the fostering of their spiritual growth, and to knowing God and his Son Jesus Christ. These holy men and women took the Gospel as their rule of life, and professed the sacred philosophy of the Cross.

This is how Saint Clement of Alexandria[59] described it to us, and it seems he had someone like Brother Lawrence in mind when he said that prayer is the primary concern of the philosopher or, better, of the Christian sage. He prays everywhere, not using many words, but secretly in the depths of his soul. He prays while walking, conversing, resting, reading, or working. He praises God continually, not only in the morning on rising and at noon as well, but in all his actions he gives glory to God, like the seraphim of Isaiah.[60]

His attention to spiritual things through prayer makes him gentle, affable, patient, and, at the same time, firm in resisting temptation, allowing neither pleasure nor pain to take hold of him. The joy of contemplation, which continually nourishes without ever satisfying him, does not allow him to experience the world's insignificant pleasures. He lives with the Lord by love, even though his body seems to be on earth. He no longer has any desire for the good things of this world because he has experienced the inaccessible light through faith, and, therefore, love has taken him where he is supposed to be. He desires nothing because he already possesses the object of his desire to the extent possible in this life.

He has no need of boldness because nothing in this life disturbs him, nor is capable of turning him away from the love of God. He does not need to compose himself because he never yields to sadness, for he is convinced all is well. He never gets angry, nor does anything move him, because he always loves God and is entirely directed to him alone. He is never jealous because he lacks nothing. He loves no one in ordinary friendship, but he loves the Creator through his creatures. His soul is completely constant, free from all change, and now he clings exclusively to God, for he has forgotten all else.

31. Permit me to add yet another stroke to this portrait from the hand of a great master who was more enlightened by the light

of an excellent faith he shared with Brother Lawrence than by all the knowledge found in the wisdom of Athens.[61] You may think it inappropriate to include masters and doctors here along with a simple lay brother, yet we find in the simplicity of his words what the greatest lights of the church have taught concerning the purity of Christian practices, and what others have drawn from Jesus Christ, who hides himself from the wise while revealing himself to the little ones.[62]

Saint Gregory Nazianzen[63] said that there is nothing more convincing or more powerful than authentic philosophy, for everything yields before the philosopher's nobility of spirit. If you deprive him of all the world's comforts, his wings lift him up and he flies to God, his only master. You cannot conquer God, nor an angel, nor a philosopher. Although composed of matter, it is as if he were not material, for he has no limits. Although he has a body, he lives on earth like a celestial being. He is impervious in the midst of so many passions. He allows himself to be conquered in everything except in the greatness of his courage. By yielding to those who think they can overcome him, he attains a place above them. He no longer clings to the world nor to the flesh. He makes use of life's comforts only when necessary. He limits his dealings to God and himself.

His soul lifts him above all perceptible things, and, like a spotless mirror, represents divine images naturally without any mixture of earth's coarseness. Every day he adds new insights to those already gained until he finally arrives at the source of light, from which source one can draw only in the next life, when the brightness of the truth has broken through the obscurity of all mysteries, and the fullness of happiness is attained. We can recognize our lay brother here, and all those like him.

32. Although Brother Lawrence lived a hidden life, all people, no matter what their personal circumstances may be, can benefit from his example as given here. He teaches those involved in the world to turn to God to ask for the grace to fulfill their responsibilities, to deal with their concerns. He teaches them to turn to God in their conversations, even during their leisure time. In keeping with his example, they will be moved to thank God for his blessings and for the good he lets them do, and ask pardon for their sins.

This is not a theoretical devotion that can only be practiced in the cloister. Everyone must adore and love God. It is not possible to carry out these obligations without establishing a heartfelt exchange that makes us appeal to him at every moment, like children who depend on their mother's constant help. This is not difficult; it is easy and necessary for everyone. In fact, the constant prayer Saint Paul enjoins on all Christians consists of this.[64]

Those who fail to do it do not recognize their needs or their incapacity for good. They do not know who they are or who God is, nor our constant need of Jesus Christ. The business and dealings of the world do not excuse us from this duty. God is everywhere, and we can converse with him anywhere. Our hearts can speak to him in so many ways, and with a little love we will not find this difficult.

33. Those withdrawn from life's struggles can benefit even more from Brother Lawrence's example. Since they are delivered from the concerns and obligations that still occupy those directly involved in the world, nothing can hinder them, in imitation of Brother Lawrence, from renouncing every thought except that of doing all things for the love of God and to give him, as Brother Lawrence said, all for all.[65]

They can surely benefit greatly from the example of his general detachment, his complete self-forgetfulness (to such an extent that he no longer thought about his salvation in order to devote himself exclusively to God), his indifference to every sort of work and occupation, and his freedom in the spiritual exercises.

NOTES

1. The description of this person suggests someone of nobility, or in any event, of high rank, who entered ("began to live") religious life ("the house of God") rather late.

2. Evocation of the Egyptian court, often a symbol of opulence in the Bible.

3. At the time of the redaction (the *Ways* received official approbation from Msgr. de Noailles on 17 November 1693), the "wrong paths" may, in Beaufort's mind, refer to Madame Guyon, and certainly to Quietism in general after the condemnation of Molinos in 1687.

4. See the General Introduction, note 16.

5. Cf. CN 1.

6. Cf. CN 23 and 32.

7. Cf. CN 4.

8. Cf. CN 1, with note 1 regarding the "forty years."

9. Cf. CN 42. The passage also recalls EL 30.

10. Cf. CN 21.

11. Cf. CN 18.

12. Cf. CN 17 and 20.

13. Cf. CN 32.

14. Cf. CN 23.

15. Cf. CN 34: "in the simplicity of his view."

16. Cf. CN 43: "continual joy."

17. Cf. CN 20 and 46.

18. On luminous faith, cf. L 11 and L 13.

19. "To reject": cf. CN 23 and 24.

20. Cf. CN 20.

21. Cf. CN 27.

22. Cf. CN 29 and 49.

23. Cf. CN 8 and 19.

24. Cf. CN 26.

25. Cf. CN 45.

26. Cf. CN 41 and 42.

27. Cf. L 1.

28. Cf. L 2

29. Cf. CN 8 and 12.

30. Cf. L 2.

31. Cf. L 12.

32. Cf. CN 12 and 29.

33. Cf. CN 16.

34. Cf. CN 21.

35. Cf. CN 16 and 31.

36. Cf. CN 12 and 22.

37. Cf. CN 6.

38. This time the "very important man" is Fénelon, who reported the visit he had with Lawrence (who was very sick), and referred to the book of the *Ways*. The exact testimony can be found in text 38 of Appendix III. See also note 18 of the General Introduction.

39. In his *Letter to Msgr. le M. de* ... (cf. Appendix II, p. 147), Beaufort placed this passage in the context of the "controversy" within the Carmelite province of Paris.

40. Cf. CN 19.

41. Cf. CN 20 and 46.

42. Cf. CN 20 and 37.

43. Cf. CN 18 and 19.

44. Cf. CN 50.

45. Cf. CN 49.

46. That is, in military life.

47. Cf. CN 48.

48. Cf. CN 21, with note 8.

49. Cf. CN 4.

50. Cf. CN 10.

51. Could Lawrence nonetheless have experienced these "kinds of things" during his novitiate, that is, "visions" and "other extraordinary things" (W 23), among which may be the ecstasy and rapture of which he spoke in the passage of CN 10, and to which Beaufort may be referring here? We think that is most unlikely (cf. our work *Vie et Pensées du Frère Laurent*). Lawrence's reservation regarding extraordinary phenomena, or experiences interpreted as such, no doubt came from St. John of the Cross, whose emphasis on faith he inherited. This reservation may have been reinforced by the relative frequency of these phenomena among his own confreres. In the *Annales* (p. xxviii of the Preface) Louis de Sainte-Thérèse, Lawrence's prior during his two years of novitiate, stated that "I have also included in this work the life of several of our deceased friars, without considering their visions, ecstasies and raptures…, [for the spirit of our Order resides] in the practice of mental prayer, penance and other solid virtues, and not in gratuitous favors from prayer, nor even in miracles which I omit for the same reason." Lawrence became the defender of purely spiritual mystical graces (without externalization, visualization or verbalization): see, for example, L 2. He recognized that "God is the master" (CN 10) even of extraordinary phenomena. The freedom and spiritual equilibrium of this humble brother are to be admired; he was filled with good sense, the sense of the essential and of the truly Divine One.

52. Cf. note 3, above.

53. Cf. Heb 1:1–2.

54. Beginning here, Beaufort repeats the narration of EL 55–59 almost literally in W 25–29.

55. Cf. Heb 10:31.

56. Cf. Eccl 1.

57. Beaufort could have been more precise: seventy-seven years.

58. In the etymological sense of "friend of wisdom."

59. Beaufort indicates "Stro. L. VII." The reference is to *Stromata*, book 7, chap. 12 ("Patrologia graeca" series, vol. 9, col. 502B–511B), of which Beaufort undoubtedly used the Latin text, with many omissions.

60. Cf. Is 6: 2–3.

61. Cf. Acts 17:16–33.

62. Cf. Mt 11:25.

63. Beaufort indicates "Or.[atio] 28" and later "Or. 29" (after the words "neither to the flesh"). The reference here is to *Oration* 26, 13, with omissions ("Patrologia graeca" series, vol. 35, col 1246; or "Sources chrétiennes" series, vol 284, [Paris: Cerf, 1981], Discours 24–26, p. 257).

64. Cf. 1 Thes 5:17.

65. Cf. L 12.

APPENDICES

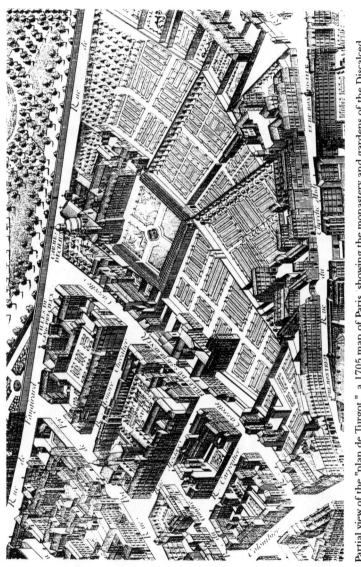

Partial view of the "plan de Turgot," a 1705 map of Paris, showing the monastery and gardens of the Discalced Carmelite Friars. (Courtesy of Father Daniel Ferrand, OCD)

Appendix I
Brother Lawrence's Monastery in Paris

After Avignon (1606), Paris was the second foundation of Discalced Carmelite friars (1611) in France, where eight monasteries of Saint Teresa's nuns were already in existence.

The first Parisian Carmelite friars acquired some fairly vast property on the Rue Vaugirard and set up a temporary chapel and some cells there.[1] In 1613 the Queen Mother Marie de Médicis, who ruled as regent while her son Louis XIII was still too young to assume authority, placed the foundation stone of the new church. "The queen was seen putting some mortar on a silver trowel, which she gracefully flung on a blessed marble stone" (Sorel, pp. 7–8). The church was dedicated to Saint Joseph in 1620; it was the first church dedicated to this saint in France, excluding the chapel of the Carmel of Pontoise (Serouet, p. 41). In 1622 they celebrated the canonization of Saint Teresa there, at the queen's expense, with a fireworks display set off from the dome of the church that caused damage in the "neighboring fields" (Hallays, pp. 21–24). The town was certainly different then from what it is today!

The construction of the monastery began in 1613. The wing on the side of the garden was built first, and occupied in 1615. "A second building was constructed in 1618, parallel to the first one, and like it, perpendicular to the church. These two buildings were later connected by two arcades that formed a cloister surrounded by arches on the main floor [i.e., the currently covered cloister]" (Pisani, pp.15–16).

When Lawrence entered in 1640 as a lay brother, the cleric brothers' novitiate was also located in Paris, but the novices must not have been numerous at that time. The *Catalogus chronologicus et historicus* (Ms 1155 of the bibliotheque L'Arsenal) mentions only one professed cleric in Paris in 1640, one in 1641 (and the lay brother Philibert at Pont-a-Mousson), and no clerics in 1642, but Lawrence is named as the only lay brother professed in Paris. The novitiate, alternately in Paris or at the monastery of Charenton (a monastery erected in 1617 near Paris, the first prior of which was a grand nephew of Calvin), remained in Paris until around 1646 before being transferred to Charenton, only to return to Paris again from 1651 to 1656.

Lawrence saw his Parisian house transformed again. "From 1674 to 1676 all the buildings were raised one floor [adding another floor]. The novitiate that was at Carrieres-les-Charenton...was moved to Paris and set up on the new floor" (Pisani, p. 16). Vocations increased greatly, and Louis de Sainte-Thérèse (*Annales*, vol. 2, p. 410) indicated that 100 friars lived in the Parisian monastery at any given time.

The monastery was large. "The Carmelite enclosure was not limited to the adjacent streets: from the Rue Cassette on the east, to the south of Rue Vaugirard...to a path on the west indicated on the plans as *sentier herbeux* [grassy path]—this was soon called "Carmelite path"—and then to the Rue du Regard. On the north the Carmelites' property bordered on the gardens that went as far as Croix-Midi, between Chasse-midy street (now Cherche-Midi) and that of the Vieux-Columbier. Two convents of nuns were built afterward on these gardens" (Pisani, pp. 7–8).

When the foundation was first established, the area was still rather isolated, "but during the seventeenth century [i.e., during Lawrence's time] the city was moving closer to them and was beginning to surround them. This was a serious concern for them. Everything that went on in the monastery was visible from the houses on the Rue Cassette and the Rue du Regard...but they had nothing to fear from the southern side. The Luxembourg park [then more extensive than it is at present] took up all of the other side on the Rue Vaugirard" (Pisani, p. 19). "To the north, at the triangle formed by the Rue Cherche-Midi and the Rue Cassette," salvation would come for the Carmelites from the foundation of two religious communities whose gardens were adjacent to that of the friars. "In 1634 the Augustinian nuns of Laon bought the land along the Rue

Cherche-Midi as far as Croix-Rouge"; this convent was known as Our Lady of Consolation. The other convent, founded from Lorraine, was that of the "Blessed Sacrament nun" Lawrence corresponded with (cf. L 13–16). "In 1653, the Benedictine nuns of the Conception of Our Lady bought the property located on the Rue Cassette between the enclosure of the Carmelites and the Rue Vieux-Colombier. Originally established in Rambervillers [where Lawrence was wounded in 1635], these nuns had to flee during the war." They moved into their Parisian convent "in 1659. They were dedicated to perpetual adoration and were called the Daughters of the Blessed Sacrament, under which name they were approved by Innocent XI in 1676 and by Clement XI in 1705" (Pisani, pp. 19–21). The congregation is no longer in existence.

The Carmelites still faced a problem regarding "the Rue Cassette on the east and the Rue du Regard on the west, where several private homes had been built. In order to ensure their privacy, the Carmelites sacrificed a part of their property to build tall houses that would serve as a screen. It was easy for them to work out the plan of the houses with their restrictions in such a way that their enclosure remained private" (Pisani, p. 21). Brother Lawrence certainly saw many things happening around him! The revenues from the houses and mansions were indeed helpful to this large community, composed of so many young men in formation; at the same time it was said that "this monastery would be the richest in the Order when the friars have discharged the debts contracted from the construction of these fine buildings" (Sorel, p. 9). This was especially true regarding the buildings constructed after Lawrence's death. The monastery was also able to profit from the revenues that came from the wonderful "Eau de Melisse," or "Carmelite Water," already being made during Brother Lawrence's time in the monastery apothecary from several types of herbs grown, among other things, in their own garden.

Let us now consider the flourishing Carmelite "province" of Paris at the time of Lawrence's entrance. Beginning with the General Chapter of 1617, "France" ("which included Lorraine and the pontifical states of Provence in addition to the national territory") was constituted a province under the patronage of Blessed Teresa of Avila (Serouet, p. 42). The new province developed rapidly. In

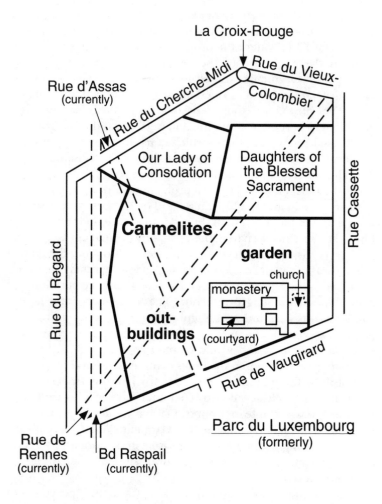

Plan of the Discalced Carmelite monastery of Paris at the time Brother Lawrence lived there.

1635 it numbered 18 monasteries, 370 professed clerics and 91 professed lay brothers (Jean-Marie de l'Enfant-Jésus, p. 39). In 1635, the province of France was divided in two: that of Avignon, and that of Paris, comprising nine monasteries of friars. Recruitment was weaker, as we know, when Lawrence entered the Order in 1640. Until 1654 there was an average of 3.2 professions each year, but during the following period, and until 1666, the average was 11.5 professions each year (Jean-Marie, pp. 47–48, did not count the professed lay brothers who constituted, as we know, 20% of the religious before 1635). In 1686, the province of "Normandy" was formed from that of Paris. The Paris province at that time numbered 303 friars, but had less than 240 when the province of "Lorraine" was created from it in 1740 (Jean-Marie, p. 49–50). The autonomous province of "Franche-Compté" was already in existence from 1653.

The Carmelites, greatly revered in the area, were still present in their monastery when, on September 2, 1792, the house on the Rue Vaugirard became the site of the horrible massacre of two bishops and twelve priests. Shortly thereafter, they had to leave because of the laws of the [French] Revolution. A part of the garden was rented to a gardener, who transformed it into an outdoor dance hall, and at the end of 1793 the house was once again taken over, but only to be used as a state prison. After the prison was evacuated, "the vacant buildings were rented... and a restaurateur rented the church and a part of the garden. They danced in the church that winter, and the altar was converted into a bar" (Pisani, pp. 51–52). In 1791, Mademoiselle [Camille] de Soyecourt, a Carmelite nun, bought a part of the house and there reorganized, as well as she could, the life of the Carmelites, until 1845, the year when Msgr. Affre, the archbishop of Paris, opened a "school of advanced ecclesiastical studies" on the site. In 1878 it was replaced by a university seminary, the present Institut Catholique of Paris. We note once again that the home of the Carmelite friars provided hospitality to Father Lacordaire and his Dominican brothers from 1849 to 1852.

A plan of the Carmelite monastery at the time of Brother Lawrence is included here on the facing page. This plan, though not altogether exact, does give a general idea of the site of the monastery. It was made from those of Pisani and Sorel, and completed by the present map of Paris. The new streets that divide the former property of the Carmelites have been indicated by dotted lines. (The little Rue Coëtlogon, and the Rue de Mezieres that extends it and now divides the property on the side of the Rue Cherche-Midi, have been omitted.)

NOTE

1. We have used Louis de Sainte-Thérèse, *Annales;* Alexandre Sorel, *Le Couvent des Carmes et le Séminaire de Saint-Sulpice pendant la Terreur* (Paris: Didier & Co., 1863); P. Pisani, *La Maison des Carmes* (Paris: Poussielgue, 1891); André Hallays, *Le Couvent des Carmes* (Paris: Bloud & Co., 1913); Marie-Joseph du Sacré-Coeur, "Historique de l'ancien couvent des Carmes déchaussés de la Rue de Vaugirard, à Paris, à l'occasion du troisième centenaire de sa fondation," *Études Carmélitaines* 3 (1913): 171–199; Jean-Marie de l'Enfant-Jésus, "Deux siècles de vie carmélitaine: La province des Carmes déchaussés de Paris aux XVIIe et XVIIIe siècles," *Études Carmélitaines* 20 (1935): 35–60; Anon., *La Maison des Carmes* (Paris: Séminaire des Carmes, 1937); Pierre Serouet, "Le couvent Saint-Joseph des Carmes déchaussés de Paris," *Nouvelles de l'Institut catholique de Paris* (1980): 34–47.

Appendix II

A Letter of Joseph de Beaufort on the "Life" of Brother Lawrence

Introductory Note to
Joseph de Beaufort's Letter

Brother Lawrence's biographer-editor was reluctantly involved in the Bossuet-Fénelon controversy. Beaufort was confessor, counselor, and one of the theologians of Msgr. de Noailles, the newly appointed archbishop of Paris, and it was in Beaufort's presence that Fénelon read the manuscript of his *Explanation of the Maxims of the Saints.* Fénelon took texts to support his own theological and mystical theses from the *Ways,* Beaufort's second book on Lawrence, which had been approved and recommended by Msgr. de Noailles. When Msgr. de Noailles and Bossuet publicly disapproved of Fénelon's book, Beaufort was obviously anxious to proclaim Brother Lawrence's orthodoxy and emphasize—or try to emphasize—the difference from Fénelon's work. That was the purpose of this "*Letter to Msgr. le M. de ...,*[1] *to serve as a defense of the Book of the Ways and Conversations of Brother Lawrence of the Resurrection, Discalced Carmelite, printed at Châlons in 1694, by the author of the book, a priest of the diocese of Paris,* in Paris, by Louis Josse, Printer to His Excellency the Archbishop, rue Saint-Jacques, 1697," duodecimo brochure, 24 pages. Thought to be lost, we have reprinted it here for the first time.

In this *Letter,* Beaufort referred in the margin to the pagination of the first edition of 1694 for Brother Lawrence's own words; we have replaced these annotations with references to our own edition. Beaufort sometimes referred as well to the pagination of Fénelon's book, but we have omitted these references because the reader has no access to Fénelon's first edition.

It is unclear whether this *Letter* belongs to Bossuet's[2] correspondence or to Fénelon's.[3] Bossuet had referred to it earlier, in a

letter dated October 14, 1697, though the letter apparently was begun on the 17th and finished on the 18th. The bishop of Meaux
[i.e., Bossuet] apparently knew about it for some time, since as of
the 14th, he had the hope that the printed letter would go out in
the same mail; in any event he was familiar with its contents, although he did use an unusual expression: "a letter *under the name*[4]
of M. de Beaufort." It seems that Fénelon was correct when he wrote
on November 19, "a letter from Monsieur de Beaufort that the
bishop of Meaux [Bossuet] had him write." What was Bossuet's part
in all this? We can imagine a first redaction by Beaufort, who would
have gathered all the relevant texts of Brother Lawrence to use in
opposition to Fénelon; this redaction would then have been reread
by Bossuet, completing the presentation of Fénelon's views, and
including forceful attacks against the Quietists.

Since Fénelon only referred to the *Ways* of Brother Lawrence,
approved by de Noailles, Beaufort never quotes the *Maxims,* the first
book on Brother Lawrence (except once by referring to the *Practice*
which is included in the *Ways*). After all, let sleeping dogs lie!

The *Letter* makes better known certain aspects of the mystical
ideal of the period as well as the fears they provoked. Furthermore,
it clarifies one aspect of Lawrence and his life. In W 17–18, Beaufort
spoke of the "natural attachment one has for the holiest places, for
one's own country" and from which Lawrence was free, since "he
took no sides." In his *Letter,* Beaufort referred to this page in the
Ways and explained that he was referring to the way Lawrence "conducted himself regarding the disputes of his Order" (see note 13).

What specifically are we to make of this? If we consider the reference to "the natural attachment to one's country" and compare it
with the reference to "the disputes of his Order," we can deduce that
there may have been a certain disagreement regarding the Lorraine
region, which, we must remember, was not French territory during
Lawrence's time. Historiographers emphasize the underlying ten-
sion caused by the question of the "subdivision of the Paris province"[5] after the provincial chapter of 1649. The issue was only partly
resolved by the creation of the province of "Normandy" in 1686.
Moreover, the Order had always been well represented in the east-
ern region of the province in the area of Lorraine. Of the eleven
monasteries of the province, four were in Lorraine (Nancy, Pont-à-

Mousson, Gerbéviller, Saint-Mihiel) and three others were nearby (Bar-le-Duc, Metz, Langres). Franche-Compté had already been an autonomous province since 1653. In fifty years the Paris province had made only one foundation, that of Lunéville in 1710.[6] In 1740, Lorraine became an autonomous province, and this decision was made at the general chapter, with 47 out of 50 votes cast in favor.

Whatever the hypothesis may be concerning the sensitivity toward Lorraine in the heart of the Paris province, Beaufort maintains that Lawrence, himself from Lorraine, was above it. And that is why the biographer could write that this citizen of heaven became "eternal like the Eternal One he had contemplated for so long" (W 17).

NOTES

1. Most likely a fictitious name.
2. See Appendix III, text 5.
3. See Appendix III, texts 6–8.
4. He uses the same expression when he speaks of the *Réponse d'un théologien* [Theologian's Response], written "anonymously" but in fact by Bossuet. See Appendix III, text 36, note 1.
5. Regarding this question, see Jean-Marie de l'Enfant-Jésus, "Deux siècles de vie carmélitaine: La province des Carmes déchaussés aux XVIIe et XVIIIe siècles," *Études Carmélitaines* 20 (1935): 46–49.
6. Lunéville: Lawrence was born four kilometers from there. A possible plan or desire for this foundation may have been the incident of which Beaufort speaks in his *Lettre* when he deals with the "controversy of his Order." See also W 15. This hypothesis suggests Lawrence's great detachment even regarding the desires closest to his heart.

Joseph de Beaufort's
Letter to Msgr. le M. de ...
[on the "Life" of Brother Lawrence]

Your Excellency [*Monseigneur*], may it please God that I might imitate the solid virtues of Brother Lawrence as easily as I will defend him to you against Quietism, whether in my own words about him or in my report of his words. I have not yet seen what was written about this little book. Yesterday I learned that Father de Chanterac brought it to Rome[1] to use as a defense for the book by His Excellency, the Archbishop of Cambrai [i.e., Fénelon]. My interest in defending Brother Lawrence obliges me to make sure you see the difference between the two.

In contrasting his book with Brother Lawrence's, I am not questioning the faith or even the sentiments of the Archbishop of Cambrai. I know he is completely orthodox. I have been aware of his integrity for too long to doubt it. I will confine my remarks to the book entitled the *Explanation of the Maxims of the Saints*. This work was hurriedly published in his absence, and therefore he may not have been able to give the appropriate attention to the revision of certain expressions, which further reflection by the author would surely have allowed him to explain properly.

His entire book apparently tends to exclude from the perfect the motivations the saints themselves used to incite themselves to the service of God, and that he assigns to the imperfect. The question hinges primarily on the virtue of hope, which he turns into a vice in beginners, because he would have it proceed from cupidity, and which he removes entirely from the state of the perfect. He teaches that we must be indifferent to the loss and deprivation of God. He also takes away from the perfect all the distinct virtues necessary to establish the only love he calls pure. Ultimately he maintains that in the most extreme trials we must renounce beatitude absolutely and deliberately sacrifice it, after reflection and with the advice of the director. This is how he interprets the greatest proof of love that can be given to God, and the greatest perfection in this life. This means that only those who actually despair are considered perfect. It is not at all an act conditioned by a kind of holy enthusiasm, as may have been the case for certain saints in the darkness brought about by the extreme nature of their suffering. The book allows for no compromise; an absolute sacrifice of salvation is required. The Archbishop of Cambrai's entire system can be reduced to this.

It is true that in order to promote this doctrine—and Christian souls will get used to it only with difficulty—they exclude only selfish, mercenary desires when they speak of indifference. It is also true that, in order to safeguard the distinct virtues, we must retain the specific motives of each, and that they say only self-interest for eternity is actually renounced in this sacrifice. But until we have defined what is meant by self-interest and selfish, mercenary desires, no one will understand these terms, in their ordinary sense, as the hope of heavenly goods, and as the equivocal terms required to express the basis of this doctrine.[2] We would have to admit that in the fifth state (that of the perfect) there is no true exercise of hope, nor prospect of the divine promises and reward; and that in the most extreme trials what we sacrifice is eternal happiness, because in hope, in the practice of the virtues, and in the very possession of God we always seek the good proper to the creature and something mercenary. This is what must be completely excluded from the perfect in order to leave only a love so subtle and pure that it reduces us to the condition of the angels and the blessed in Heaven.

Let us see if what I wrote about Brother Lawrence can serve to support this doctrine and whether it conforms to it. But before examining this, it must be noted that neither Brother Lawrence nor myself give any rules whatsoever regarding the spiritual ways. Please note that I am reporting only the particular experiences of a perfect soul, and that we do not mean the same thing in saying that, in the state of indifference, one cannot (without becoming imperfect and lacking in grace) admit any selfish desires—that is, according to what the Archbishop of Cambrai says, to have a view to one's own salvation and beatitude. This is against the express teaching of the Council of Trent.[3]

There is certainly a great difference between excluding the desire for salvation in every case for all kinds of people, and interpreting the disposition present in a particular individual who, at certain times, may not be concerned with the thought of his salvation but who, nonetheless, continually strives for it by his actions.

When someone speaks only for himself, nothing is more appropriate than interpreting his words by his actions, and those of Brother Lawrence show us that no one was more concerned about his salvation than he, even at those moments when he said he wasn't thinking about it. His whole life, according to what he said about himself and his advice to others, gives evidence of a constant vigilance over his thoughts, words and actions. It was his understanding of the need for penance and atonement for sin, as he himself stated, that made him enter religious life (W 14). The life he chose was one of the most penitential in the church. The fact that he embraced this way of life and persevered in it in complete fidelity for more than sixty years[4] indicates he was certainly concerned about his salvation and desirous of heaven, and that he was indeed aware of his sins.

We must continually keep watch over ourselves, he said, so that we don't do, say, or think anything during illness that might displease God in an attempt to relieve the sufferings (L 15). If something like that occurs we must humbly ask pardon of God for it and do penance. When he fell into some sin, he confessed it to God without excusing himself (CN 22). He turned to God so that he would not fall back into the same sin and asked only that he be spared from offending him (CN 30). To say that we do not think about our sins is merely to say, as did Brother Lawrence, that we no longer worry about them and no longer go over our past confessions.

Brother Lawrence advised everyone to do what he himself did all his life, namely, to engage in a continual conversation with God, asking for his help before undertaking any activity. He recommended asking pardon for the sins we acknowledge having committed, and giving thanks after any good we may have accomplished (W 8). He refers to many different kinds of acts here besides those of thanksgiving, unlike the Archbishop of Cambrai's book that says nothing about this.

Everything is possible for one who believes, he said, still more for one who hopes, and even more for one who puts these virtues into practice. There are only faith, hope and love to cultivate (CN 51). Here we find the three virtues necessary for every Christian in any state of life; but each is preserved as distinct, and not just in its particular motivation.

In keeping with the apostle's teaching, this holy friar truly used all his strength in the practice of love, the most excellent of the three,[5] without excluding the other two. The love to which the Quietists would like to reduce all virtue is an idle love that accomplishes nothing and is compatible with all the comforts and consolations of life. The "forgetfulness of virtues and of all motivation" practiced by the saints is according to them [i.e., the Quietists] a real and genuine forgetfulness, which only produces an idle love.

In what way can we compare this with Brother Lawrence who, with his many acts, with the exercise of all the distinct virtues, and with the asceticism of his life as a Discalced Carmelite, was one of this world's men most opposed to the false mystics? When the Quietists, who give us written lessons[6] concerning the highest form of perfection—though they have carefully eliminated all physical mortifications—have lived a life comparable to that of Brother Lawrence, then they may be permitted to say that they are not mindful of their salvation nor of their past sins. This type of discourse is truly suspect in those who live an easy life in the midst of the greatest distractions of our times. But we can tolerate it without fear of illusion in the lives of those who practiced continual penance, and whose lives have been an exercise of all the virtues, because their actions interpret their words.

On occasion, Brother Lawrence may not have thought specifically about heaven or hell; nonetheless, he used all the means the saints practiced and taught to reach the one and avoid the other. But you will not find in him, or in me, the disastrous exclusion of beatitude that would introduce a language foreign to the Gospel, reduce all religion to metaphysical abstractions, and degrade the most outstanding saints by lowering them to the rank of the imperfect.

What would become of the Gospel, where we find none of these abstruse expressions? Would Jesus Christ, who calls all to perfection, have hidden the means from us by not teaching us to renounce the desire for beatitude? He who proposed it throughout as the final end for which we were all created, and even implanted this intense desire in our hearts?

Would only those who knew how to make this subtle abstraction be perfect? "God wants me to desire him as my good, my happiness, and my reward, but he does not want us to desire him *for the specific reason* that he is our reward, our salvation, etc."—without this precise detail, according to this new approach, I would always remain imperfect, that is, while I ask God for the eternal Kingdom he promised me....

The perfect, according to the whole of Sacred Scripture, desired only the possession of God and renounced all the attractions of their times to acquire him. At least this was the case until the metaphysicians introduced the subtlety of their precisions into the religion of Jesus Christ.

What can be said of David, who had no knowledge of this kind of language, but rather incited his heart to observe God's law by the hope of reward?[7] Moses likewise would only be ranked with the imperfect, because, as Saint Paul taught us, this holy lawgiver of the Jews had the possession of God in view.[8] All the martyrs, who in the most heroic act of love, as Jesus Christ himself said,[9] gave their lives for God, would be nothing more than imperfect because they did not learn that they had to renounce all kinds of desires, even the possession of God, and therefore they died explicitly asking for eternal life. But Saint Paul himself, who desired his own dissolution in order to be with Jesus Christ,[10] and who hoped for the crown of justice from the just judge[11]—what rank would he have obtained according to these new mystics since he forgot to ask for his reward according to the precise motive, namely, that he would not desire it as his reward? Was it to find something comparable in Brother Lawrence that they had the Archbishop make the trip to Rome?[12]

If, however, there are bishops who are opposed[13] to this new way of speaking and who want to preserve the sacred deposit of religion in the holy simplicity of Scripture and Tradition, if they want to prevent the establishing of Christian perfection in the ways of extraordinary prayer while maintaining it in the observation of the Law, where Jesus Christ put it, then they will let the whole world know that prayer is in danger; as if this great gift of God could not be preserved without this new science of abstractions! God keep us from being intimidated by these threats. The children of Saint Benedict, of Saint Bernard, of Saint Teresa, of Saint Francis de Sales and of so many others would no longer share in the spirit of prayer. Is there no more perfection and true prayer in any of our holy monasteries, in penitents of either sex, because in following the example of their pastors, they closed their ears to these novelties?

By the grace of God, you will find nothing like this in Brother Lawrence, nothing that resembles Quietism. I maintain that no one in that sect would profess this doctrine if they had to live as he did. Let us see if he conducted himself in his great suffering according to the rules of the book of the *Maxims of the Saints* for souls who are experiencing trials.

"Whether I be damned or whether I be saved, at least I want to continue loving God until the end of my life" (CN 12). What Brother Lawrence believed is evident here. It is as if he said, "In the situation where I find myself, I am hard pressed to convince myself that I could avoid hell. But, on the other hand, given my love for God, I cannot believe he would want me, or allow me, to be lost. What can I do in this darkness except continue to do what I have been doing all along? I will continue to love God with my whole heart." He turned the trials God sent him into a holy diversion, though this is assumed to be impossible, and sanctified them by the exercise of his love. This was surely a sacrifice and an abandonment in trust, in keeping with the maxims by which this man of God was nourished. He explained them by saying that the trust we have in God honors him greatly and draws upon us great graces (CN 33); and this principle also supported him in his anticipation of another suffering when he said, "My greatest trial would be to lose the perceptible awareness of God, but his goodness assures me I will never lose it totally" (CN 38). His indifference was only toward bodily pains and the other events of life, as one can see by the conduct he maintained regarding the disagreements within his Order,[14] and in an affair for which he had worked a long time, the outcome of which he saw reversed in an instant (W 15).

This is in no way comparable to an absolute sacrifice, to agreeing to the absolute loss of God, after reflection and with the consent of the director, or to what would be required of a soul in its ultimate trials. You might say that only self-interest is sacrificed and that nothing essential for salvation is meant here. Nonetheless, it would be quite a sacrifice to make this renunciation the most heroic act of pure love and the final step toward perfection. No, the whole system requires us to renounce beatitude and, in a word, to make a true act of despair. This is exactly what Brother Lawrence did not do, nor would he have wanted to attain perfection under these conditions. He preferred to trust in God rather than to renounce the possession of him forever.

It is true that this good man was familiar with mystical texts, and he sometimes borrowed their terms to express what was occurring within him. Thus we must interpret him by his actions, by the way he lived his whole life. Neither he nor I intended to give anyone any rules in this little book, nor did we agree to speak according to the extreme exactitude of scholasticism.

As for me, I am an insignificant man, and if what I wrote—before the prelates gave their rules, in the thirty-four articles,[15] for correcting the abuses in the mystics' language—was responsible, I won't say for disturbing the church, but even for causing the slightest concern, because I may have used less than accurate terms, I declare to you, Your Excellency, that without waiting for a formal censure, I would be ready to correct myself on the first warning given. After writing about the inner dispositions of a saint I would at least try to imitate his humility.

Since what I said concerning this fine friar was authorized by so outstanding a prelate,[16] I fear no censure. He saw nothing there that did not conform to the teachings of the most moderate mystics, and he knew how to eliminate all the ambiguous terms. Brother

Lawrence's life will interpret his expressions, will prove him blameless before those who will judge them fairly, and will always distinguish him from all the extreme mystics. On this day, the 18th of October, 1697.

APPROBATION

I have read this little work wherein the author, himself pious and enlightened, explains himself with as much clarity as soundness on a delicate matter subject to misinterpretation. Given at the Sorbonne, November 6, 1697.

PIROT

Extract from the King's Approbation

By the grace and favor of the King, given at Paris, this seventh day of November, 1697, signed, Boucher. It is permitted to Louis Josse, publisher of His Excellency the Archbishop, to print, sell and produce: *A Letter to Msgr. de M. to use as a defense of the book of the Ways and Conversations of Brother Lawrence of the Resurrection, Discalced Carmelite,* and this for a six-year period beginning the day of its printing; with prohibitions to whom it may concern, to print, to have printed, to sell or produce the here-mentioned letter without permission, under penalty of confiscation of the forbidden copies and a fine of fifteen hundred francs, including all the expenses, damages, and interest as is justified by the here-mentioned privilege.

Registered in the book of the Communauté des Librairies et Imprimeurs, Paris, November 8, 1697. Signed, P. AUBOIN, Syndic.

Printed for the first time November 15, 1697.

NOTES

1. Father de Chantarac defended Fénelon's interests in Rome. "Yesterday" refers to October 17, 1697, since the letter is dated the 18th.

2. [The French text here is somewhat obscure, but Beaufort is clearly objecting to misleading terminology.]

3. A note in the margin by Beaufort: "Session 6, chapter 16." Cf. Denzinger 809.

4. Beaufort rarely corrected his chronological inaccuracies. Lawrence persevered in religious life for fifty-one years, not "more than sixty."

5. Cf. 1 Cor 13:13.

6. In the margin, Beaufort wrote "Moyen Court," the book by Madame Guyon.

7. Beaufort wrote "Ps 119" in the margin, a reference to Ps 119 (118):12.

8. Beaufort wrote "He 11" in the margin, a reference to Heb 11:26 (118):12.

9. Beaufort wrote "Jn 15, 13" in the margin.

10. Beaufort wrote "Ph 1" in the margin, a reference to Phil 1:23.

11. Beaufort wrote "2 Ti 4, 8" in the margin, a reference to 2 Tim 4:8."

12. Cf. Note 1.

13. Beaufort was thinking specifically of Msgr. de Noailles, Bossuet, and Godet des Marais (Chartres), who had disapproved of Fénelon's book. See Appendix III.

14. In the margin, Beaufort refers to page 20 of his book, the *Ways*. This page begins with the words "approached that of the Blessed," and ends with "found God everywhere." See W 17 and the Introductory Note for Appendix II.

15. The reference is to the important "Thirty-Four Articles of Issy," signed on March 10, 1695 at Issy by Bossuet, Msgr. de Noailles (still bishop of Châlons), Fénelon, and the theologian M. Tronson, the Superior General of St. Sulpice.

16. Msgr. de Noailles, his bishop.

Appendix III

*Brother Lawrence
in the
Fénelon-Bossuet Controversy*

Introductory Note to
Texts on Brother Lawrence
from the Fénelon-Bossuet Controversy

We have spoken several times in this work of the connection that existed, before and after his death, between Brother Lawrence and Fénelon. At the time of the great dispute between Bossuet (supported by Msgr. de Noailles, whose vicar general, Beaufort, had edited the works of Brother Lawrence) and Fénelon over his book *Explanation of the Maxims of the Saints,* the archbishop of Cambrai [i.e., Fénelon] often quoted Brother Lawrence as one of the many authorities who were supposed to support his doctrine of Pure Love, which in the perfect is above any mercenary spirit, any self-interest. Fénelon quoted—and somewhat mischievously, as Bremond observed—Lawrence's *Ways and Conversations,* a book strongly recommended by Msgr. de Noailles. In so doing he always used the indirect testimony of Beaufort, the biographer, rather than the first-hand material of Lawrence's own writings, found in the first volume, that of the *Maxims.* It is also evident that Fénelon rarely mentions what would appear to be the most characteristic of Lawrence's themes, namely, life in the presence of God.

We have gathered here all the passages we were able to find dealing with Brother Lawrence. Some were part of Fénelon's writings; some were from his opponents, de Noailles and the even more scornful Bossuet. Seen in context, these passages recall Madame Guyon (the Parisian woman Lawrence would certainly have heard of toward the end of his life) and the drama of Fénelon, who seems to deserve to be exonerated, three centuries after the unpleasant events of 1694–1699.

Texts on Brother Lawrence from the Fénelon-Bossuet Controversy

1. The first mention of Brother Lawrence in Fénelon's writings is found in his *Mémoire sur l'état passif* [Treatise on the Passive State],[1] dated the end of July, 1694.[2] At the end of the *Mémoire*, Fénelon mentioned "the Life of Father Lawrence,"[3] after Balthasar Alvarez, John of the Cross, Catherine of Genoa, Angela of Foligno, Tauler, Marguerite of Beaune, Surin, Francis de Sales, Thomas of Jesus, Aquaviva, and Mother [Jeanne] de Chantal.

NOTES

1. *État passif: Preuve de cet état tiré de l'Écriture, des Pères et des Saints des derniers siècles, pour répondre aux objections de M. de Meaux.* This text was published in Jeanne-Lydie Goré, *La Notion de l'indifférence chez Fénelon et ses sources* (Paris: PUF, 1956), pp. 194–243. Lawrence is mentioned on p. 242.
2. Fénelon spoke of this work in a letter dated July 28, 1694 to Bossuet (cf. X, 29). The "Issy Conferences" had just begun.
3. "Father": *sic*, at least in Gore's edition.

2. There are packets of yet unedited texts collected by Fénelon "either at the time of the Issy Conference or with his *Explication des Articles* [Explanation of the Articles] in mind." Perhaps they were collected to compose or to defend the *Maximes des Saints* [Maxims of the Saints] that contained "a certain number of passages taken from the Fathers, and from ecclesiastical and spiritual authors used

to support his doctrine of Pure Love."[1] Brother Lawrence is found in packet five among the "testimonies of the Saints on abandonment and on the truth of extraordinary trials,"[2] and in packet nine containing "diverse extracts."[3]

NOTES

1. Albert Cherel, *Fénelon: Explication des Articles d'Issy, publiés pour la première fois par Albert Cherel* (Paris: Hachette and Co., 1915), p. 161.
2. *Ibid.*, p. 166.
3. *Ibid.*, p. 168.

3. Early in February 1697, Fénelon published the work that would be at the forefront of the controversy: *Explication des Maximes des Saints* [*Explanation of the Maxims of the Saints*]. The bishops of Meaux (Bossuet), Chartres (Godet des Marais) and Paris (de Noailles) opposed it, and so Fénelon appealed to Pope Innocent XII in a letter dated April 27, 1697. A commission of theologians was set up in Rome; after long deliberations, opinions were evenly divided (five for and five against). In the meantime, on September 15, 1696, Fénelon published an *Instruction pastoral sur le livre intitulé: Explication des Maximes des Saints* [Pastoral Instruction on the book entitled: *Explanation of the Maxims of the Saints*]. This Instruction dealt with the perfection of love, and Brother Lawrence is quoted as follows (II, 320–321):

> Brother Lawrence of the Resurrection, a Discalced Carmelite Friar, whose way of life was described by an ecclesiastic of singular merit in a little book approved by his Excellency the Archbishop of Paris, said, "since I entered religious life (these are his own words) I no longer think about virtue or my salvation" (W 11).
> This Brother said that "he never swayed from his determined goal in spite of the terrible sufferings he had for four years, so terrible that no one could convince him of his salvation" (this is the suffering I called invincible, and the impression of despair that does not destroy hope).
> "Without thinking about what would become of him and without concerning himself with his sufferings—as troubled

souls would do—he consoled himself by saying: Come what may, at least I will do everything for the love of God for the rest of my life. Therefore, by forgetting himself, he resolved to lose himself for God, and this worked to his advantage" (W 13). These words would be impious if they were not understood to mean merely the exclusion of self-interest or natural, mercenary interest, the only kind of renunciation called for in my book. This is clearly what the holy friar meant. "He sometimes wished he could hide from God what he was doing for his love so that, renouncing all reward, he would have the pleasure of doing something purely for God" (CN 11). Did this fine friar want to forego his reward and uproot hope from his heart? Certainly not; but the love that possessed him and made him exercise acts of hope ordinarily leaves no room for natural self-love or self-interest regarding promised blessings. He insisted that he "was always governed by love, with no other interest, with no concern whether he would be damned or saved (CN 8); that he was greatly troubled in spirit, thinking that he was surely damned, and that no one in the world could have convinced him otherwise" (CN 12). He was mistaken when he said he was "surely damned," as the scrupulous are; he only imagined it were true. He added that "he thought neither of heaven or hell; that his whole life was freedom and continual joy." I have never before come across such strong language. Moreover, I cannot praise the prelate enough who sanctioned such naive expressions where innocence, disinterested love, and the joy of the Holy Spirit stand out. The author of the book said, "And so Brother Lawrence began by the more perfect way, leaving everything for God and doing everything for his love. He thought neither of heaven or hell" (W 11).

4. Did the Archbishop of Paris contradict himself by approving Brother Lawrence, as Bossuet did in approving Father Surin's *Fondements de la vie spirituelle* [Foundations of the spiritual life]? Fénelon's blast had many echos, as Bossuet attested in a letter dated October 7, 1697 to his nephew in Rome, Father Bossuet, who defended his interests (Bossuet's *Oeuvres*, VI, 369):

> The two books the archbishop of Cambrai sent to Rome
> have caused quite a stir. The one authorized by the archbishop

from Paris [i.e., de Noailles], then bishop of Châlons, is, I believe, Brother Lawrence's book about which we have already spoken. The other, which I approved as dean of Metz, is called *Fondements de la vie spirituelle* [*Foundations of the Spiritual Life*], which they claim is replete with the new spirituality. In fact, it amounts to nothing, and the completely opposite position is found in the passage they urge against me, chapter 5, which I point out to you just in case, so that, if it falls into your hands, you will know what it is.

Keep me informed; nothing is insignificant. If the plots are serious in Rome, know that the same is true here, but we still have the King and Madame de Maintenon. I will let the archbishop of Paris and the bishop of Chartres know what you tell me.

5. In a letter dated October 14, 1697, to his nephew in Rome, Bossuet was the first to speak about Joseph de Beaufort's *Letter to Msgr. le M. de ...* [see Appendix II above], even before its publication (Bossuet, *Oeuvres*, vol. 6, p. 375). We have spoken about it at length in the Introductory Note to Appendix II, pp. 137–139.

Remember Brother Lawrence, whom they reported to the archbishop of Paris. You may receive a letter about this from that Ordinary under the name of Beaufort. It is well done and you can circulate it, should the subject of that little book ever come up.

6. Beaufort's *Letter to Msgr. le M. de...* [cf. Appendix II] was published on November 15, 1697; on November 19, Fénelon communicated some very revealing details to Father de Chanterac, his defender in Rome (IX, 244):

You will have seen a *Letter* from Father de Beaufort that the bishop of Meaux [i.e., Bossuet] had him write, and which they sent to Rome. The purpose of the *Letter* was to defend Brother Lawrence and show that his writings do not conform to my book. The same Monsieur de Beaufort wrote me a letter of apology on this subject that I will send to you.

You will see, first of all, that in his printed letter he said nothing precise or conclusive that would indicate any difference between his book and mine regarding the term "self-interest for eternity," and consequently my position remains intact; secondly, that the letter he wrote reveals an ashamed, embarrassed man who recognizes his mistake.

I suppose it is the responsibility of the Roman Church, the one judge in this incident, to impose silence on the parties involved while awaiting a judgment. Put yourself in my place. This is painful, but I will let them crush me even though I possess the means necessary to confound these obviously slanderous accusations.

7. In a communication to Father de Langeron on December 10, 1697, Father de Chanterac acknowledged receiving Beaufort's *Letter* (IX, 267–268):

Sir, I have found the copy of Monsieur de Beaufort's *Letter* in the package you sent on November 23. It is easy to see he was not the original author, or else his style is entirely new. He neither explained nor defended the book *The Life of Brother Lawrence,* but rather he condemned the archbishop of Cambrai's book. Both could be equally good or bad, so the important thing was to point out that his expressions were very different from those of the archbishop of Cambrai. For if they were similar, you could always compare them with each other and maintain they teach the same errors and present the same illusions, if, fortunately for him and for us, it were not already certain that reasonable persons could only understand the meaning of these expressions in their ordinary sense, which is good and very holy, since they express the sentiments that grace gave to this outstanding servant of God. Furthermore, sir, I do not remember speaking about this book; at least I am certain I never showed it to anyone, and it is entirely possible, without judging rashly, that it was not so much Beaufort's fear that made him write such a long, fine letter, overnight, as the desire of some other person to make him explain publicly or rather to explain himself in opposition to the archbishop of Cambrai's book.... I also know the Nuncio forwarded Beaufort's printed letter; I am also certain the Nuncio's letter said nothing either in favor of or against it.

8. Four days later, on December 14, 1697, Father de Chanterac (LX, 271) acknowledged to Fénelon that he received Beaufort's "printed" *Letter* as well as the "handwritten" one addressed to Fénelon (cf. supra, text 6). In Rome it was thought that Monsieur Boileau, the Paris theologian, played the greatest role [in writing the *Letter*]. According to this letter, Fénelon would have written an answer to Beaufort that apparently was not preserved:

> Your Excellency, I received your last package of November 19, with both the handwritten and printed versions of Monsieur de Beaufort's letter. Our friends, who had already sent me a copy, indicated to me that they did not think he wrote it, or that at least Monsieur Boileau played the greatest role in it. In fact, it was only written to publicize the harm of your book; but in no place do they show how your expressions are different from those they approved in Brother Lawrence's work. That was the only thing it dealt with, and that is what they tried to justify. The shame of which it gives evidence should bring about, it seems to me, admirable fruits of penance. Your reply is the most appropriate way to deal with the issue and to provide instruction.

9. In the meantime (August 6, 1697), de Noailles, Bossuet and Godet des Marais published their *Déclaration des trois Évêques* [Declaration of Three Bishops], objecting to Fénelon's book. Fénelon therefore drafted his *Réponse de M. l'archevêque de Cambrai à la Déclaration de M. l'archevêque de Paris, de M. l'évêque de Meau et de M. l'évêque de Chartres, contre le livre intitulé: Explication des Maximes des Saints* [Reply of the Archbishop of Cambrai to the *Declaration* of the archbishop of Paris, the bishop of Meaux, and the bishop of Chartres against the book entitled *The Explanation of the Maxims of the Saints*]. Brother Lawrence is mentioned several times. Here is the first passage (II, 335):

> When His Excellency the archbishop of Paris approved the *Life of Brother Lawrence* composed by his fine vicar, in his own home, he approved saying that this friar "forgot himself and was resolved to lose himself for God, ...that he no longer thought of virtue or his salvation (W 11 and 13), ...that he was always governed by love without self-interest (CN 8)." If "interest" is es-

sential to hope, these words mean that he was "always governed" without hope. Would you not have to condemn this despair rather than approve of it? Would you have "to recommend the reading of this book to all those who seek to acquire a true piety" [quoted from the *Approbation* of the book], as a book that "will truly help them?" Would you need to propose Brother Lawrence as a model of perfection who "wished he could hide from God what he was doing for him so that, renouncing his reward, he might have the pleasure of doing something purely for God" (CN 11)? These are the most absolute renunciations of self-interest. They cannot be considered temporary acts accomplished by simple abstraction. This is a state that lasted about forty years. This prelate did not identify the absolute, constant exclusion of self-interest with the renunciation of the desire for salvation and Christian hope. He maintained the real difference between these two things. I have only proposed what he approved in the life of so many saints. And what these authors say about interest without the addition of any qualification, I have said about self-interest alone, that is as property [*propriété,* "proprietariness"] that is unanimously rejected as an imperfection by all the contemplative saints of the last centuries. Why do you accuse me of a crime? Why do you confuse self-interest with salvation in my book, charging me with the most impious despair?

Once you understand that "self-interest" and "selfish motivation" in my book refer to a natural, imperfect affection for the promised gifts, as it is understood by the approved authors, then all the difficulties that result from these equivocal expressions regarding interest disappear. According to the Fathers and other saints there are just people who are still *mercenary.* There are others more perfect, who are no longer *mercenary* but who are purely *children.* This mercenary quality the Fathers eliminate from the perfect is self-interest, which I also eliminate in them.

10. From the same reply of Fénelon (II, 342):

Why is it that the three prelates always insist on confusing in my book what they clearly distinguished in the books of Father Surin and in the life of Brother Lawrence? Why do they conclude by the use of parentheses that the *desires for salvation are necessarily mercenary?* Did they not say themselves, on page 21, that the motivation *for eternal life as reward* (which, according to the Council of Trent, must be *attributed even to the perfect,* in imitation of the example *of Moses and David*) does not make us *mercenary,* but fashions *children who by love are fond of the paternal heritage?* If this motive offers nothing mercenary to the soul it incites, then it is not mercenary by its nature.

11. From the same reply by Fénelon (II, 344):

I have never wanted anyone to be indifferent to salvation, but only indifferent to self-interest, which is very different from salvation, and which two of the three prelates have distinguished from salvation when they approved the writings of Father Surin and Brother Lawrence. This self-interest is only the satisfaction of a natural love of ourselves; these are *the remnants of the mercenary spirit,* as I have expressly said....

12. From the same reply of Fénelon (II, 346):

When Saint Francis de Sales bore "for so long the impression of damnation...like a sentence of certain death, where he had to come to this terrible resolution, since in the next life he was supposed to be deprived forever of loving a God so worthy of being loved, he wanted at least, etc.," the *impression of damnation,* and what is described as *like a sentence of certain death* followed by a *terrible resolution* was only, in my opinion, an *involuntary impression* of despair, an *apparent but not an innermost belief* [*conviction apparente et non intime*]. We can explain this in more precise terms. When Brother Lawrence, whose life was approved by the archbishop of Paris, said that "during the emotional sufferings he had for four years, so great that he was certain he would be damned, and no one could have convinced him otherwise, etc." (W 13), and when they reported these even stronger statements, *that he was convinced he would be damned,* etc. (CN 12), this certitude, which would have submitted to no authority in the world, cannot be more favorably explained than by calling it an *apparent but not an innermost belief,* an *involuntary impression* of despair. Even when Job, the model of tested souls, said, *I am in despair,* he had an *involuntary impression* of it, since he spoke truthfully. Therefore he must have had some kind of *apparent but not innermost belief.* This is what the prelates themselves stated and even approved in works other than my own. This is what they condemned, however, in my book.

13. From the same reply of Fénelon (II, 347):

How is it that these prelates confuse eternal happiness with *self-interest for eternity* in my book, when they know so well how to distinguish these things, and have even approved this distinction, in the writings of Father Surin and Brother Lawrence, where *self-interest,* even when *divine* and *for eternity,* is excluded as an imperfect motive?

Regarding simple consent: in my book it only has to do with *self-interest for eternity,* which I distinguish from salvation, saying that *we must always desire the effects of God's promises in ourselves and for ourselves.* My words should not be interpreted in any way contrary to their clear restrictions. Must they charge me line after line with the most extreme and impious contradictions, for fear that they might approve in my book the distinction between salvation and *self-interest* that they approved in Father Surin and in Brother Lawrence? These prelates have accepted the *apparent but not innermost belief* as a true belief, and *self-interest,* which I have always distinguished from salvation, as salvation itself.

14. From the same reply of Fénelon (II, 348):

In the *Life* of Brother Lawrence it is written: "For four years Brother Lawrence's sufferings were so intense that he was certain he would be damned and no one in the world could have convinced him otherwise": therefore it was useless to present the dogma of faith to him. He found peace in saying: "Come what may, I will at least do everything for the rest of my life for the love of God" (W 13). Here is undoubtedly only an *apparent belief* in condemnation in which only *self-interest* or the consolation of eternal self-love in regard to eternity is sacrificed, and in which the innermost belief in *mercy* and the *desire for the fulfillment of the promises in oneself and for oneself* is preserved. This state, far from admitting any despair, is the perfection of natural hope.

15. From the same reply by Fénelon (II, 350):

Did not the bishop of Meaux [i.e., Bossuet] approve these words in Father Surin? "The soul eliminates even good desires, except the particular desires that God gives it for the things that are his will.... When it pleases God that the soul do something, he gives it a peaceful desire that does not prejudice it to this indifference.... This soul does not consider at all its spiritual treasure." This is the rejection, not of all good desires, but of intense, natural desires not given by grace. Excluded here is the *self-interested preoccupation to assure that one is virtuous, and to enjoy one's virtue as one's own.*

When Brother Lawrence spoke as follows: *Since I entered religious life*—that is, for about forty years—*I no longer think about virtue or my salvation* (W 11), he did not stop practicing more faithfully than ever all the virtues appropriate to his state in life; but without thinking about the fact that they were virtues, he practiced them to accomplish the will of God and did not seek therein self-interest or natural self-love. This example indicates *whether or not I have imposed this on the spiritual masters,* as the prelates have so accused me, when I said that they declared at times that they were no longer seeking virtue for its own sake. I spoke like Saint Francis de Sales who said: "How blessed are those who strip themselves of even the desire for the virtues and from the concern of acquiring them, only wanting them to the extent that eternal wisdom will communicate the virtues to them and will use them to acquire them." Thus the three prelates have me say that the holy mystics excluded from the perfect state *the practice and the acts of virtues.* 1. I did not say one word about *acts;* thus they accuse me without grounds. 2. I never spoke of the *practice,* but only *practices of virtue.* So little have they read the mystical authors of which I am speaking that they cannot be accustomed to the great distinction these writers make in their ordinary language between the *practice* or the essential exercise of the virtues and the *practices of virtue,* which are only, according to them, *an arrangement of formulas to convey a biased testimony.*

16. In addition to their joint declaration, the "three bishops" spoke individually against Fénelon's book, which merited them the faithful reply of the Archbishop of Cambrai. First of all, here are the

passages where he spoke of Brother Lawrence in his four letters on the *Pastoral Instruction* of Archbishop de Noailles [of Paris]. The extracts come from the *Premiere Lettre de Monseigneur l'archevêque de Cambrai à Monseigneur l'archevêque de Paris, sur son Instruction pastorale du vingt-septième jour d'octobre 1697* [First Letter of His Excellency the Archbishop of Cambrai to His Excellency the Archbishop of Paris, on his Pastoral Instruction[1] of October 27, 1697] (II, 477):

> What can you condemn in the Quietists, Your Excellency, that I have not already also condemned more strongly? Will you deny any one of the things I thought had to be admitted in good faith? Will you say that souls undergoing trials experience no apparent, imaginary belief of condemnation? Saint Francis de Sales, Blessed Angela of Foligno, Brother Lawrence, so many other saints, and even so many of the scrupulous do not allow us to conceal it.

NOTE

1. *Instruction pastorale de M. l'archevêque de Paris, sur la perfection chrétienne et sur la Vie intérieure, contre les illusions des faux mystiques.* This can be found in Fénelon's *Oeuvres*, II, 420–466.

17. From the same *Premiere Lettre* [First Letter] of Fénelon to Archbishop de Noailles (II, 480–481):

> Let us now deal with the book done by your order, under your eyes, in your house, and by your fine vicar who had your complete confidence[1] for so many years.
>
> You have said of this book: "We recommend the reading of it to all who seek to acquire true piety" [quoted from the *Approbation* of the *Ways*].
>
> Your Excellency, be the judge in your own case; with the gravity of the sanctuary, weigh my expressions, on one hand, and those, on the other, of this book you have made your own by proposing it as the rule of perfection for all pious souls. You reproach me for an "invincible belief." But didn't Brother Lawrence say (W 13) "that the terrible sufferings he had for four years had been so great that no one could have convinced him that he was saved," etc.? This belief that no one could take

from him, and that he could not dispel himself even by listening to all the people in the world, is this not invincible? The author adds that this friar "had never swayed from his determined goal; but without thinking about what would become of him"—What an expression! What, no reflection for four years about his salvation, even though he thought he was lost, nor about his eternal damnation that he supposed was certain? How would this appear to you, Your Excellency, if you were to read it in my book?—"and without concerning himself with his sufferings as troubled souls would do, he consoled himself saying: Come what may...." Is this the consolation you would propose as a model *to all those who seek to acquire true piety?*

If they think they are lost, or have become lax, or hardened, or have fallen into condemnation, would you advise them to console themselves instead of sighing, and would you exhort them to say: *Come what may?* Brother Lawrence added: "I will at least do everything for the rest of my life for the love of God. Thus, forgetting himself, he resolved to lose himself for God, and this worked to his advantage" (W 13).

What do these words mean? *He was resolved to lose himself for God? To be willing to lose yourself for God,* when you think you *will be damned,* is this not accepting your damnation? I never spoke like this. I have taken care to say precisely the opposite. Brother Lawrence's acceptance of his eternal damnation seems yet confirmed by what follows.

"He was," says the author, "always governed by love with no other interest, without caring whether he would be saved or damned; ...certain that he was damned" (CN 8, 12). Here is a sure belief in his damnation, and he wasn't concerned about it. Not to be *concerned* about something that you think you have *certainly* lost is not to desire it at all; for you would desire it if you were concerned about it. He no longer desired his salvation, they will say, because he no longer cared about it, because he was *certain* he was lost. Have I ever said that a soul completely *certain* of its damnation could *not be concerned at all* about its salvation? Have I ever approved this disposition for any reason whatsoever? Nevertheless, Your Excellency, you present Brother Lawrence as a model for pious souls; for four years he was *not concerned* about his salvation, *certain he was damned,* and "always governed by love, with no other interest, without worrying whether he was damned or saved" throughout his long life in religion. This disposition was established in him for about forty years. The author affirms he *thought neither of heaven or hell,* and he presents this disposition as the most eminent perfection. He said that "Brother Lawrence began, by the more perfect way, thus leaving everything for God and doing everything for his love; he no longer thought about heaven or hell" (W 11).

You might say this friar was ignorant and that he explained himself very badly. But we would reply that it was the responsibility of the author to correct his expressions, and that you were supposed to ensure this when you authorized the book. The question was whether this friar had preserved Christian hope and the desire for salvation. A great archbishop and a venerable priest assumed responsibility for his expressions when they said that Brother Lawrence thought he was *surely damned, without worrying* whether he was or not, and that this disposition is *more perfect.* They have not inserted at this point the corrections with which my book is filled. It was never said that Brother Lawrence's belief was *only apparent* and not *innermost;* nor that it was only an *involuntary impression of despair;* nor that in this *apparent belief* he always desired God's promises; nor that he *sincerely desired his mercies;* nor that he learned from his director that we are *never permitted to believe we are damned.*

If you say, Your Excellency, that this friar's belief was only *apparent,* and not from the innermost depths of his *consciousness,* you will be correct. But you will be obliged, in order to explain Brother Lawrence, to use the corrections that are found in my book. You will also be asked whether these corrections are natural enough for Brother Lawrence.

The author said, *believing for certain that he was damned.* Whoever speaks of *believing for certain* speaks of more than an *apparent* belief. When Brother Lawrence *did not worry whether he would be damned or saved;* when *he was willing to lose himself for God;* when he said *come what may,* he expressed an unqualified consent, and this consent can only result in the thing of which he is speaking, his condemnation, which he presumed to be *certain.*

He can only be excused by the qualification of *self-interest,* about which he never said a single word, but which good faith and the principles of spiritual books require to be understood throughout. It is not a question of saying, as was recently written,[2] that Brother Lawrence did penance for many years to bring about his salvation. This reply does not resolve the difficulty. Brother Lawrence, it could be said, could have done penance like many others and still have been deceived. The issue here is his doctrine and his internal acts, and not his external practices. Moreover, the only way of answering me is to show by means of the book that Brother Lawrence was not detached from his *self-interest regarding his eternity;* for it is on the term *self-interest* that I insist. If Brother Lawrence had no *self-interest regarding eternity* for so many years, not even when he was convinced of his damnation, *this self-interest* can be sacrificed, for Brother Lawrence never had any in his heart, however perfect he may have been. Only the term *interest* can justify the *Life* of Brother Lawrence, the author who wrote it, and the prelate who approved it. It is evident that Brother Lawrence's dispositions are confined to not seeking this *self-interest* or *mercenary spirit* in salvation; it is in respect to this that he *was willing to lose himself* and was *not concerned* at all *whether he was saved or damned.* Therefore nothing would be more unjust than the rigorous criticism of these expressions of this soul so moved by the love of God. But the key that explains and saves the work you have approved with praise is not stated in clear terms in the book itself; you must take them from mine.

NOTES

1. Beaufort was de Noailles's confessor.
2. Allusion to Beaufort's *Letter to Msgr. le M. de...;* cf. Appendix II, p. 143.

18. From the same *Premiere Lettre* [First Letter] of Fénelon to Archbishop de Noailles (II, 493):

In a word, Your Excellency, all the trouble comes from your insisting that the elimination of the *mercenary* quality or self-interest is, in my book, the elimination of supernatural hope or the desire for beatitude; rather I have always maintained, along with the Fathers, that self-interest, or this mercenary quality, was only a natural imperfection that the perfect overcome. I will not repeat the example of Brother Lawrence here in order to spare you the suffering that this decisive example could cause you.

19. In his *Réponse de Monseigneur l'archevêque de Paris aux quatre lettres de Monseigneur l'archevêque de Cambrai* [Reply of His Excellency the Archbishop of Paris to the four letters of His Excellency the

Archbishop of Cambrai], which can be found in Fénelon's *Oeuvres*, II, 519–538, Archbishop de Noailles explained the reasons why, having complete confidence in Brother Lawrence, he approved his works (cf. II, 535–536):

> We must conclude this, Your Excellency, for my letter is already too long and I am afraid it has tired you. Nonetheless, I cannot pass over two articles to which you have so strongly urged me to reply. Your desire will be satisfied. I will answer with a yes and no, since you desire it so much. It is true that I approved the book of the *Ways* of Brother Lawrence. However, I do not need *to take the key point of natural desire from your book to explain or to save it*. No, Your Excellency, that would be a poor resource. This key point was never found in your book, and given what you have done with it since, it can serve neither Brother Lawrence, nor you, nor anyone.
>
> This is how I thought we were to explain the expressions of this fine friar. Since he was led by the way of love, the simple thought of the divine perfections was almost always adequate to sustain him in the greatest works of penance and in the most terrible anxieties regarding his salvation. He did not always need to reflect specifically on the joys of paradise or on the pains of hell. Nonetheless, do not think, for this reason, that his so pure love excluded, as in the new mystics, either the multiplicity of the various acts of religion or the love and the practice of all the virtues of his state. You only have to read his *Life* again. No one could beseech God more for his salvation than he did. No one could have been more vigilant. No one was ever less indifferent to possessing God or losing him. Then where does the statement, found in the book, that he was not concerned about heaven or hell come from? This statement certainly needs some explanation. The deeds of this holy friar explain it. Since we wrote it at a time and place where the disputes incited by the new mystics did not require the precision that we are supposed to use now, we did not think that those willing to profit from every opportunity would abuse this language. Brother Lawrence's long, rigorous penitential practices, his exact, continual vigilance over himself, makes us easily understand that when he had said in his own informal language that he did not care about his salvation, he meant to say, according to the original meaning of the term, that he had *no worries,* that

is, no anxiety about his salvation. The anxiety, the solicitude that Scripture wants to spare faithful souls precisely expresses Brother Lawrence's meaning. It is inconceivable that a Discalced Carmelite, so faithful to his *Rule,* was indifferent to his salvation, for which he acted and suffered continually for so many years.

What then did he mean when, tempted and believing he was damned, he cried out: "Come what may, I will at least do everything for the rest of my life for the love of God?" Was this not accepting damnation? No, Your Excellency, nowhere in Brother Lawrence will you find this impious consent to eternal condemnation, this despair of your souls undergoing trials. He was far from it. You have only to *weigh for yourself with the seriousness of the sanctuary* the entire passage you quote, on the one hand, and your expressions, on the other. This fine friar, when afflicted with thoughts of his damnation, far from consenting to them and yielding to despair, as your perfect ones would do in the last trials, *consoled himself* by turning his mind away from the negative ideas that troubled him and applying himself to the divine love that reassured him. "Come what may, I will do everything for the love of God."

It is true, as you have so often repeated, that no one could have convinced him of his salvation during those four years of temptation. Yet the word of God reassured him. "My greatest trial would be to lose the perceptible awareness of God." But his goodness assured [him] that "I will never lose it completely." He could not believe that "God could let a soul that abandoned itself completely to him suffer for a long time." He was not among those souls bent on despairing, those *who will not listen to the reassuring dogma of faith.*

Anyone who understands the human heart so well, it seems to me, would have immediately understood Brother Lawrence's language in his sufferings. It is the pious diversion of a mind that wisely seeks to ward off troublesome thoughts. The best way to dissipate a dangerous temptation is not always to attack it head on. The images that should be erased are sometimes imprinted more strongly by direct resistance, so it is safer to turn the mind promptly to other objects. When Brother Lawrence was tempted to believe he was damned, *he did not pay attention to his suffering,* says the author you criticize, *as troubled souls would do;* and that is called fighting the temptation by not paying attention to it.

Does this mean, as you would maintain, that he consented to the loss of his eternal well-being? Did Brother Lawrence deliver himself invincibly over to despair according to the method of the newly perfect? His disposition was entirely different. He found *consolation,* on the contrary, in an even stronger resolution to love God and to serve him throughout his life.

He knew full well, Your Excellency, that nothing is more incompatible with the acceptance of damnation than the truth, and the works it produces. He had learned this truth from St. Paul. Therefore, when Brother Lawrence said, like St. Francis de Sales, "Come what may, I will love God all my life," that is to say most effectively, whatever my present distress may be, I will possess God in heaven, since I want to love him always on earth; in no way did he consider sacrificing either *the supernatural or the natural desire for salvation.* He decided to assure his beatitude by taking the safest means to arrive at it. He threw himself into the bosom of love, the inviolable sanctuary against divine vengeance. For what Christian does not know that God never condemns those who love him, and that he prepares his eternal kingdom for those who perform their deeds to please him?

20. Fénelon replied in Latin—for the letter had to serve in Rome—to Archbishop de Noailles, with *Responsio illustrissimi D. Archiepiscopi cameracensis ad epistolam illustrissimi D. parisiensis archiepiscopi* [Response of His Excellency, the Archbishop of Cambrai, to the Letter of His Excellency, the Archbishop of Paris] (II, 538-554), a true résumé of the issue. There are two allusions to Brother Lawrence, who is ranked among the "perfect" (II, 551 and 553). The Latin reply interests us also in terms of what it says about the discreet role of Lawrence's biographer-editor, Monsieur de Beaufort, after the publication of Fénelon's book, *Explication des Maximes des Saints* [*Explanation of the Maxims of the Saints*]. Beaufort's name appears six times in the *Responsio,* which quickly followed the letter Fénelon received from Archbishop de Noailles, already printed on May 28, 1698 (cf. II, 538). We have translated several passages:

It is not surprising if, preoccupied by countless serious concerns, you have forgotten or obscured certain circumstances.

But I, the only one truly affected by all this, keep everything either faithfully recorded in my memory, or very carefully noted in my manuscripts as in a journal. First of all, the foundation of this is the letter containing the twenty questions that we have discussed together. It was in the month of February, 1697, when my book was first attacked. At that time you did not oppose any of the twenty questions. That was the time you should have rejected them, if they appeared false. (II, 538)

Here follow the twenty questions, of which some of the passages are translated from the original French, published in II, 252–253: *Vingt questions proposées à M. de Paris par M. de Cambrai, en présence de Madame de Maintenon et de M. le duc de Chevreuse* [Twenty questions proposed to the Archbishop of Paris by the Archbishop of Cambrai, in the presence of Madame de Maintenon (the wife of King Louis XIV) and Monsieur the Duke of Chevreuse].

XIII. Is it not true that His Excellency the Archbishop of Paris examined my work with Monsieur de Beaufort in my presence, reading it very carefully the first time; that he then kept it nearly three weeks; that he made an extract from his observations and marked the places he thought called for revision for the sake of greater prudence; and that I revised them in my room at Versailles, in his presence, in such a way that he said I may have made the corrections too rapidly?

XIV. Is it not true that he then went to see Monsieur Tronson who for his part examined my book for six weeks, and that they together concluded it was *correct and useful?*

XV. Is it not true that I again asked His Excellency the Archbishop of Paris what doctor he wanted to reexamine my work; that I offered to submit it to the examination of Monsieur Boileau whom he thought was too biased to do it for me; that he finally gave me Monsieur Pirot, who, having examined my work to the point of refusing to keep it to examine it any longer, praised it lavishly? I still have the letter from His Excellency the Archbishop of Paris, who pointed out Monsieur Pirot's praises to me.

21. In February 1698, the Bishop of Meaux [Bossuet] once again attacked his former friend Fénelon in his *Préface sur*

l'Instruction pastorale donnée à Cambrai le 15 de septembre 1697 [Preface to the Pastoral Instruction given at Cambrai on September 15, 1697]. It is not Bossuet who will become Brother Lawrence's promoter (Bossuet, *Oeuvres*, V, 739):

> Shall I say a word about Brother Lawrence, the Discalced Carmelite, for whom so solid a reply has been given? I can only state one of this fine friar's ideas. He said he thought it was "impossible for God to let a soul completely abandoned to himself, and resolved to endure everything for him, suffer for a long time" (CN 33). He thought it was impossible? Is this a dogma that he had in mind? No, he was speaking out of sentiment, and not dogma; this dogma was inaccurate, as the long sufferings of Job and the other saints bear witness.
>
> Nonetheless, this sentiment, based on the immense goodness of God, was admirable. But if he thought it was impossible for God to permit a soul that endured hardship for his love to suffer for a long time, could he have believed that God would allow it to suffer eternally? He did not believe it; and what he said about his damnation was the effect of both an overly scrupulous conscience and an imagination overwhelmed with its suffering.
>
> But his sufferings "were so intense for four years that no one could have convinced him of his salvation" (W 13); and that is, Fénelon says, "the suffering I called invincible, and the impression of despair that does not destroy hope." What a difference there is between the issue and the person. On one hand, a lay brother who admits his suffering, and on the other, a doctor who establishes a dogma. The brother speaks of a temptation in his imagination that he cannot overcome; the theologian adds the belief and the conviction that are not acts of the imagination, and they are both invincible. In order to explain this more clearly, "the belief" that he admits is "intentional"; it is consequently an act of the higher part and of which the imagination is incapable. This fine lay brother never thought of this, nor of absolute sacrifice, simple consent, nor any other deliberate acts that would make despair complete.

22. In May 1689, Fénelon replied through five *Lettres de M. l'archevêque duc de Cambrai à M. l'évêque de Meaux, en réponse aux divers*

écrits our mémoires sur le livre intitulé: Explication des Maximes des Saints
[Letters from His Excellency, the Archbishop, Duke of Cambrai to
the His Excellency, the Bishop of Meaux, in response to the various
writings or statements on the book entitled the *Explanation of the
Maxims of the Saints*] (containing Bossuet's *Preface*), of which an extract from the fourth letter is given here (II, 599):

> Brother Lawrence, says the author of his *Life* (CN 11),
> "sometimes wished he could hide from God what he was doing
> for his love, so that, receiving no reward, he would have the
> pleasure of doing something solely for God." As for me, I never
> said that the perfect, *if it were possible, would not want God to know
> that they loved him.* I only said the following: "We would love God
> as much, even if, by some impossible supposition, he did not
> know we loved him," etc. The saints are, according to your own
> admission, *full of these impossible suppositions.* I only make them
> in keeping with their example, to express, as they do, a love in-
> dependent of the motives that are excluded by these supposi-
> tions. But did I ever say that these souls did not want God to
> know their love for him? There is a great difference between as-
> suming—impossible as this is—this lack of knowledge in God
> so that we can desire to love him according to this supposition,
> and indeed truly wanting God to be unaware of this. Here is a
> statement taken from St. Francis de Sales that is even stronger
> than mine: "If we could serve God without merit, which is im-
> possible, we should desire to do so." He speaks in the same
> manner when he says: "If it were possible for us to be as pleas-
> ing to God by being imperfect as by being perfect, we should
> desire to be imperfect, for in this way we would foster in our-
> selves the most holy virtue of humility."
>
> Is it permissible to charge me with a statement so different
> from what I affirmed? Was it necessary to change my text and
> the meaning of my words to charge me with the impious doc-
> trine of the renunciation of the desire to please God? You say
> "this is also the first thing our author intended." You must ask
> Brother Lawrence's author if this fine friar *intended* to renounce
> *the desire to please God.*

23. Bossuet did not let this pass, and responded with a *Réponse
de Monseigneur l'Évêque de Meaux à Monseigneur l'Archevêque-Duc de*

Cambrai [Reply by His Excellency the Bishop of Meaux to His Excellency, the Archbishop-Duke of Cambrai] (Bossuet, *Oeuvres*, V, pp. 753–777). This merited him on Fénelon's part three *Lettres de Monseigneur l'Archevêque de Cambrai pour servir de réponse à celle de Monseigneur l'Évêque de Meaux* [Letters from His Excellency the Archbishop of Cambrai serving as the reply to that of the Bishop of Meaux]. Here is an extract from the first *Letter* (II, p. 635):

> Father Surin, the approbation for whose works you renewed in your last volume written against me, affirmed that "the soul continually abandons everything to the extent of forgetting itself, its life, its health, its reputation, its glory, its time, and its eternity.... This is accomplished when the person has entirely renounced himself in all his human and divine interests." He added that this soul "tries to see where the Lord's glory is, with no consideration for its interests." He did not even take the precaution I took of adding "own" to the term "interest." He said furthermore: "leaving behind all its interests..., and having no concern for its well-being, not only in time, but even in eternity..., the soul's main concern is to take care not to act out of consideration for its interest and to never settle for any motive other than that of pleasing God. It is not that I criticize the motive of reward, which can sometimes be useful and helpful; but the most praiseworthy and desirable motive is that of the glory, the love, and the good pleasure of his God."
>
> Brother Lawrence was "always governed by love, with no other interest, without worrying whether he was damned or saved" (CN 8).
>
> You ask for *one single example*, Your Excellency. I present a great number, taken from the best authors in the spiritual life. All these authors absolutely exclude "interest" from the perfect life, especially when the term "own" is added to that of "interest." If they had understood God's beatifying activity as part of the interest they exclude, they would have excluded hope, and placed perfection in despair. Why do you speak this way...?

24. And from the second *Letter* (II, 641):

> You reinforce your position by saying that these terms "persuasion and belief naturally have to do with the mind and the

higher part of the soul." Must I contradict you in everything? I
am sorry that I have to do it so often, but I cannot avoid it on
this occasion. *Persuasion,* in our language, no longer means *to
believe.* Brother Lawrence *certainly believed he was damned* for four
years (W 13). A *certain belief* indicates more than a simple *persuasion,* especially when it is constant for four years. Would you say
this *certain belief* was from the *higher part of the soul?* According to
you, St. Francis de Sales had *an impression of condemnation…like
a sentence of sure death. He presumed that he would no longer love in
eternity.* To *presume* something in this way is not to be *persuaded*
of it, especially when this *supposition* goes as far as formulating a
terrible resolution founded solely on the very supposition. To *presume* something in this way is to posit it as certain and to make it
serve as a foundation for everything that you resolve.

But do you want to see an expression incomparably stronger than mine? It comes from the holy father Blosius, approved
by so many famous universities in Germany and the Low Countries, and greatly praised by Cardinal Bellarmine. It is stated by
Father Surin. Thus you have approved it. "Then," he says,
"speaking of trials, the person is completely left to himself. *Hic
jam homo totus sibi relinquitur.*" He does not say that the person
appears abandoned; he simply says that the person is so. "He
thinks he is wasting his time. *Totum etiam tempus suum se perdere
putat.* He thinks he has lost everything." Note that he does not
say: the person *imagines.* He does not take this precaution; he
says the person *believes.* Listen again to the holy writer: "Thus
having fallen into such extreme sadness and horrible despair,
he says: 'It happened to me, for I was lost and deprived of the
light; all grace was withdrawn from me.' "

25. As we have already seen, Fénelon was not reluctant to repeat himself! From the same *Letter* (II, pp. 642–643):

> Consider Brother Lawrence a bit more. His *certain belief* that
> he was *damned* lasted four years, and during these four years *no
> one could have convinced him otherwise;* undoubtedly he could not
> convince himself either. This is an *opinion* or *persuasion,* for they
> are the same; he goes so far as to say a *certain belief,* but so *certain*
> and so *invincible* that this fine friar could not overcome it, *nor
> could all the people in the world* have freed him from it, for this
> belief was indeed *invincible.* It was not, however, in the *higher part*

of the soul; it was completely *invincible,* but only *apparent* or imaginary, that is, precisely as I described it in my book.

You ask me why I did not say in my book, as I am now saying, that this belief is only imaginary. Your Excellency, do not alter my text and you will find in it everything you say is lacking. Recognize that the *persuasion,* according to my book, is only *apparent,* and admit that *apparent* and *imaginary* are exact synonyms. Furthermore, the holy authors I have quoted did not make these qualifications. Blosius said the soul *believes that it has lost everything* and *is itself lost.* He did not say the soul imagines it; he said that it falls into a *horrible despair.* Brother Lawrence was *certain,*[1] said the author of his *Life;* he did not say that he imagined he believed it. You yourself, Your Excellency, have said that St. Francis de Sales *assumed he would no longer love in eternity;* you did not say that he imagined he assumed it. Furthermore, if you had attacked St. Francis de Sales, Blessed Angela of Foligno, Blosius, Mother Marie of the Incarnation, Brother Lawrence, Father Surin, and all the other holy contemplatives on their expressions, they would have replied as I did. They would have said that their *beliefs,* or *assumptions,* or *persuasions* were only apparent. If you were attacked for your quotations of their words, you would defend yourself by saying that you only intended to establish by this a belief that *is not innermost,* but only *apparent* or imaginary. The more they pressed you, the more you would seek all the terms necessary to clear up your adversary's misunderstandings. This is exactly what I am doing with you. So please note that the issue in everything I say about trials is the separation of the higher part from the lower. I place all the *anxiety* and *obscurity* in the lower part alone. I place all the peace and the complete exercise of the virtues in the higher part.

...What will become of us, if we can no longer say, *without excusing Molinos,* that very innocent souls have an imaginary or *apparent belief* in their damnation?

St. Francis de Sales *assumed that he would no longer love in eternity!* Brother Lawrence certainly "believed this for four years, to the extent that no one could have convinced him otherwise." Must those who have so strongly attested to these facts now recant them, for fear of defending Molinos? Is not the best way of explaining this kind of *persuasion* to say that it was only *apparent* or imaginary, and by assuring that it was a *problem of scruples?* Have you forgotten all the facts you yourself stated? Must you deny them for fear of providing the Quietists with ammunition?

God's truth does not need our lies. We would allow the fanatics to triumph if we concealed these experiences, supported as they are by the writings of so many saints. In assuming these facts, we would very easily confound the Quietists.

NOTE

1. Further on (II, 646), Fénelon will repeat the texts of Blosius, Lawrence and Surin on their feeling of incertitude regarding their salvation.

26. One can never be clear enough, as Fénelon came to see in his third *Letter* to Bossuet (II, pp. 656–657):

I am taking this notion of sacrifice from your own book where you explain St. Francis de Sales. *He bore in his heart a sentence of sure death;* he bore an *impression of damnation,* and this is where he made a *terrible resolution.* By *terrible* we mean something that costs nature a great deal. It means an act whereby a significant attachment is sacrificed. Therefore you affirm that so *disinterested* an act would conquer the devil. Why was it so *disinterested?* It was so because it excluded some form of interest, and therefore disinterested and free from self-interest mean the same thing. This resolution is so *terrible* in that it is so *disinterested,* that is, it renounces some form of interest. Call this interest what you like; instead of saying sacrifice, say renunciation or elimination; all the names are the same to me provided that the basis of the thing remains incontestable. What is certain is that St. Francis de Sales renounced this interest by this *terrible* act. This renunciation is not conditional. The act is not only called disinterested, but he even called it *so disinterested.* He therefore totally excluded this interest.

You have even called this *terrible* renunciation a *kind of sacrifice.* Here are your own words: "God moved him, by special inspirations, to make him this kind of sacrifice, according to the example of St. Paul." It is true that in your statement you confused, as you generally do, the sacrifice of *troubled souls* with that of St. Paul, which is very different since it was made without the apostle appearing troubled about his salvation. But here is a *kind of sacrifice,* in your opinion, that *troubled souls* can make with their director's advice. And when can they do it? Is it only apart from suffering, when they have a hope they can sense, and when they see clearly that it is only a question of an impossible case? On the contrary, it is when they suppose like St. Francis de Sales *that they will no longer love in eternity;* it is when they are certain, like Brother Lawrence, that they will be *damned,* to such an extent that *no one in the world could convince them otherwise* (W 13); it is when, to speak like Father Surin whom you approved, they *see themselves obviously offensive and unbearable to themselves.* Here is the *kind of sacrifice* you say that *God incites* the soul to make.

Let us find this sacrifice, Your Excellency, in your own words. You say, explaining Father Surin, he that rejected an *anxious concern.* This *anxious concern* is therefore completely eliminated or sacrificed, in your opinion. This *anxious concern* has the quality of being *mercenary,* which the Fathers admit in the imperfect just ones. In my opinion, it is a *remnant of the mercenary spirit* that can be absolutely eliminated. It is this same *mercenary* quality or *remnant of a mercenary spirit* that I thought could be most naturally translated by the term *self-interest.* What you call a *terrible resolution,* an act *so disinterested,* a *kind of sacrifice,* is undoubtedly an absolute and unconditional renunciation of the *anxious concern* regarding God's gifts.

The archbishop of Paris spoke like you when he explained Brother Lawrence "who was always governed by love, with no other interest, without worrying whether he would be damned or saved" (CN 8). This prelate affirmed that the word *worry* was an old-fashioned word that meant an *anxious desire,* which had in fact to be renounced. We must then, according to this prelate, renounce or completely sacrifice the *concern* or the *anxious desire* for salvation. I have found this concept of absolute sacrifice in the Fathers, in St. Francis de Sales, and in your own works. Why do you then accuse me of inventing it, as though it is *found in no other author,* of *making of it my idol* and the dearest object of my most perfect spirituality; of even having it *serve as a pretext* for the false *mystics* who teach despair, and *whose cause I shrewdly took up?* Thus you accuse me of supporting the books of Madame Guyon, when I only say what you yourself recognized as obvious equivalents.

27. In June, 1698, Bossuet published his *Relation sur quiétisme* [Report on Quietism], in which Madame Guyon is called "this Priscilla" who "found her Montanus to defend her," namely Fénelon

(cf. section XI, 8; Bossuet, *Oeuvres,* VI, p. 115). Deeply wounded, the Archbishop of Cambrai reacted in July with a *Réponse à l'écrit intitulé: Relation sur le quiétism* [Reply to the work entitled: Report on Quietism]. There he retraced his spiritual journey of recent years. Though he recognized the weaknesses of Madame Guyon's mystical formulations, he reaffirmed his esteem for her. Here we find some highly favorable lines on Lawrence:

> This person [Madame Guyon], it is true, seemed very pious to me. I admired her greatly; I believed her to be very experienced and enlightened in the ways of the interior life, although she was very unlearned. I believe I have learned more about the practice of these ways by examining her experiences than I could have done by consulting very learned, though inexperienced, people.
>
> We can always learn by studying God's ways in those, who, though unlearned, are experienced. We could certainly have learned the practice of the presence of God by conversing with Brother Lawrence, for example. This is what I could have said to His Excellency the Archbishop of Paris and to the bishop of Meaux in Monsieur Tronson's presence. I will never retract what I said....

28. Bossuet was not appeased, and wrote his *Remarques sur la Réponse de M. l'Archevêque de Cambrai à la Relation sur le quiétisme* [Remarks on the Reply of His Excellency the Archbishop of Cambrai to the Report on Quietism], thereby provoking Fénelon's *Réponse de Monseigneur duc de Cambrai aux Remarques de Monseigneur l'Évêque de Meaux sur la Réponse à la Relation sur le quiétisme* [Reply of His Excellency the Archbishop Duke of Cambrai to the Remarks of His Excellency the Bishop of Meaux on the Reply to the Report on Quietism] (III, pp. 53-88). During the summer of 1698, the relentless Bossuet ("Bos assuetus aratro"!) composed three treatises in Latin —for the benefit of Rome (*Mystici in tuto, Schola in tuto,* and *Quietismus redivivus*) that he published in *De nova quaestione tratatus tres* (Bossuet *Oeuvres,* VI, pp. 1–109). Fénelon responded with two long letters (III, pp. 189–233). He then published a new book, a collection of numerous texts from various spiritual authorities with

a view toward supporting the principal affirmations of his controversial work, the *Explanation of the Maxims of the Saints*. The work was entitled *Les principales Propositions du Livre des Maximes des Saints, justifiées par des expressions plus fortes des saints Auteurs. Avec un avertissement sur les signatures des Docteurs et sur les dernières Lettres de M. l'Archevêque de Cambrai* [The Principal Propositions of the Book of the *Maxims of the Saints,* supported by the strongest expressions of the holy authors. With a note on the Doctors' signatures and on the last letters of His Excellency the Archbishop of Cambrai] (III, pp. 248–308). One of the "authorities" in this book, and generally the most recent, was "the *Life* of Brother Lawrence, approved by His Excellency the Archbishop of Paris" (III, p. 260). Lawrence is quoted here six times: in regard to pure love (III, p. 260; from W 11); in regard to the conditional sacrifice of eternal beatitude (III, p. 268; from W 13, CN 12); in regard to the possibility of an invincible belief of being condemned by God, but which does not proceed from the innermost depths of the conscience (III, p. 268; from CN 8, 12); in regard to humble abandonment, full of wisdom, to the present moment God gives us (III, p. 285; from CN 23, 34–35); in regard to the love of God's will and the practice of all the virtues without thinking about the fact that they are virtues (III, p. 287; from W 11); and in regard to pure love, the only motive for all our acts (III, p. 292; from CN 11, 8, 12; W 12; CN 26, 29).

29. Bossuet did not like Fénelon's book at all, and he took advantage of the opportunity to express himself in *Les Passages éclaircis ou Réponse au livre intitulé: Les principales Propositions du Livre des Maximes des Saints, justifiées par des expressions plus fortes des saints Auteurs. Avec un avertissement sur les signatures de Docteurs et sur les dernières Lettres de M. l'Archevêque de Cambrai* [The Clarified Passages or Reply to the book entitled: The Principal Propositions of the Book of the Maxims of the Saints, supported by the strongest expressions of the holy authors. With a note on the Doctors' signatures and on the last letters of His Excellency the Archbishop of Cambrai] (Bossuet, *Oeuvres,* VI, pp. 226–249).

Bossuet intended to simplify the discussion by seeking a "rule to evaluate the exaggerated expressions" (VI, p. 232):

The author of the new system who based his arguments on the evidently exaggerated passages should have presented this rule, for otherwise he would overstate or understate the extreme expressions as he pleased, and thus he would compose an arbitrary system. What he would not do, or could not do, I will do for him. Here is the rule: Whenever impiety, blasphemy, or obvious errors against the foundations of the faith are attributed to those considered saints, we must believe this is an exaggeration, and oppose whatever contains error or leads to it. The rule is as simple as it is sure; otherwise we would have foolhardy saints, blasphemers, those who stray from the principles of the faith, and this is impious and contradictory.

I trust in Our Lord that the very proposing of this rule will begin to open the eyes of the wise reader regarding the majority of the passages of the new system. And when he hears the saints or pious spiritual men and women, for example, a Blessed Angela of Foligno, a St. Francis de Sales, a Louis Blosius, and if you like, a Brother Lawrence and the others, speak only of a horrible despair, and yet wanting to love, do penance, and continue to serve God until the end—though they believed themselves damned or wanted to be—this is clearly an obviously exaggerated impulse. But in order to correct these ideas and only accept those that are certain, I will give some principles for resolving all these passages, obviously derived from this rule.

30. Although Brother Lawrence found himself in very good company, the inserted qualification "if you like" was not a good sign, when Bossuet, in the *Passages éclaircis* [Clarified Passages], (VI, p. 237), applied his "rule" to Lawrence, after first evaluating Blessed Angela of Foligno and, second, St. Francis de Sales (or more accurately, a *Life* of the saint by the bishop of Évreux):

> The third writer is Brother Lawrence. We will then consider Brother Lawrence whom we have so clearly explained so many times. "He was always governed by love, with no other interest, without worrying whether he would be damned or saved."
>
> "He was deeply distressed, believing he was surely damned, and no one in the world could have convinced him otherwise.... This suffering lasted four years.... Since that time he thought neither of heaven nor hell. His whole life was nothing but freedom and continual joy."

This authority is so important that it is repeated three times, so much is it relied on. And it is added: "that he sometimes wished he could hide from God what he was doing for his love, so that, receiving no reward, he would have the pleasure of doing something purely for God."

Reply—In a word, excess and exaggeration are evident throughout in the sayings of this fine friar; he believed he was damned, without losing, however, this complete security about which we have spoken in detail in keeping with the Fathers; everything is resolved by this response.

But what exactly did he mean when he said he was not concerned about heaven and hell? Another word will explain it. He did not worry at all about them, for that would accomplish nothing; and—God forbid—this would be to declare oneself superior to David and Moses, as well as St. Paul who praised them. He was not worried about his salvation at all, about taking care of it, solely, principally, finally. This is what he meant, for he felt that we should forget ourselves, rather than forgetting God, who was dearer to him than he was to himself. This is not disputed. Anything beyond this cannot be understood literally without foolish error. "His life," he said, "is freedom and continual joy"; without anxiety, without difficulty, he is freer and more content than the rest of the world.

Moreover, as overstated as these passages are, I do not see here, or in the others for that matter, the absolute sacrifice, or the impossible accomplished, or the absolute incapacity to reason, or the simple consent to his just condemnation, or the other expressions that lead to the inaccuracy of the new system, where they supposedly improved on the most exaggerated expressions.

31. In no way did this reassure Fénelon, who unburdened himself in his two *Lettres de Monseigneur l'Archevêque duc de Cambrai à Monseigneur l'Évêque de Meaux en réponse à l'ecrit intitulé: Les Passages éclaircis* [Letters from His Excellency the Archbishop Duke of Cambrai to His Excellency the Bishop of Meaux in response to the work entitled: The Clarified Passages], (III, pp. 309–335). In general Fénelon reacted this way: "The tradition and language of so many saints are evaded in your *Réponse* [Response] by these three words: *exaggerations, loving madness.* This is how you explain all the

masters of the spiritual life. If you wanted to explain them, you should have at least sought a more serious explanation worthier of them" (III, p. 309). As for Lawrence in particular, there certainly were things to correct, which he did in the second letter (III, p. 325):

> What you have called a *belief of the imagination,* I have called an *apparent persuasion.* This imaginary belief thus seems to be a certainty. This is why Angela of Foligno said: "Although I may be damned, I will do penance." And again, "Seeing myself damned, I am not at all worried," etc. This is why she added that "if all the wise ones in the world and all the saints in heaven wanted to console her" by taking away this imaginary (and so distressing) belief, she could not even *believe them.* So she cried out, "Know that I am rooted in a despair the likes of which I have never known because I have completely despaired of God and of all his benefits: ...I am assured," etc. This is why St. Teresa declared that all the admonitions of her director accomplished "nothing because the understanding was so darkened that it was incapable of seeing the truth, but only believing what the imagination represented to it, which is thus the mistress." This is why Blessed John of the Cross said that "the soul sees more clearly than the day, etc. It finds neither consolation nor support in any spiritual doctrine, nor spiritual master, because, no matter what reason is given to it, it cannot believe it." This is why Blosius described for us a soul that "believes no awareness of God is possible for it..., that believes it is wasting its time..., that believes it has lost everything." This is why St. Francis de Sales "in an impression of damnation...made the terrible resolution, *saying* that in the next life he was to be deprived forever," etc. You will not find even the shadow of a conditional expression in these terms. This is why Brother Lawrence, who walked in the footsteps of so many saints, said that his "sufferings had been so intense that no one in the world could have convinced him of his salvation." The author added to the words of the pious solitary, "He was certain he was damned and no one in the world could have convinced him otherwise."
>
> Say as often as you like that your reply regarding Brother Lawrence can be stated "briefly, namely that excess, exaggeration are evident everywhere in the sayings of this fine friar; that he believed he was damned without losing, however, this complete security." Truly, Your Excellency, you treat too lightly what

lies beyond your reckoning and is unanimously accepted. To listen to you, the *Life* of Brother Lawrence is so full of such outrageous and scandalous exaggerations that it must be abandoned in spite of its approbation. But we see that this great contemplative walked in the footsteps of so many other saints that you would not dare abandon so openly.

32. In the same letter (III, 328), Fénelon again used Brother Lawrence to support his doctrine of pure love:

What is certain is that the desire to draw [God's] graciousness and generosity upon us can be mixed with some self-interest, and it is this self-interest that the saints tried to eliminate without ever thinking about excluding the conformity of our will to God's, or the graciousness found there. It is in this sense that Brother Lawrence said (CN 11) "that he sometimes wished he could hide from God what he was doing for his love, so that, receiving no reward, he would have the pleasure of doing something purely for God." As for me, I did not say, as he did, that *we would desire to be able to hide from God, etc.* I only said, that *if, were it possible, God did not know, etc., we would still love him.* You may scorn these simple sayings and these loving considerations that I thought had to be attributed to the expressions of the saints, who, without offending dogma, tended to exclude all that would encourage self-interest in the virtues; as for me, I try to explain, and I reverence in the saints, the language of their love.

33. At the end of 1698, Rome had not yet made a pronouncement on Fénelon's controversial book. On December 23, Louis XIV wrote an impatient letter to the Pope asking for "a prompt decision on the archbishop of Cambrai's book" and the eradication of "the root of the evil" (cf. IX, p. 647). Bossuet made a list of propositions taken from Fénelon's book to be censured by the Doctors of the Sorbonne. Fénelon defended himself with his two *Lettres de Monseigneur l'Archevêque duc de Cambrai à Monseigneur l'Évêque de Meaux, sur les douze Propositions qu'il veut faire censurer par les Docteurs de Paris* [Letters from His Excellency the Archbishop Duke of Cambrai to His Excellency the Bishop of Meaux on the twelve

Propositions he wanted to have censured by the Doctors of Paris]
(III, pp. 372–404). Fénelon tried to support the propositions. Concerning the second proposition on pure love free from self-interest,
he quoted (III, p. 379) Brother Lawrence once again, who had been
approved, we must remember, by Archbishop de Noailles [of Paris]:

> What will you say in reply to the sayings of the venerable
> Brother Lawrence? We would have thought that you might at
> least have spared from your censors the one who approved the
> life of this admirable solitary. Although the saints of past ages
> could not temper your censures, we naturally did not think you
> would want the Doctors to condemn, in the sight of their prel-
> ate, the expressions whose reading he recommended to all
> those seeking to acquire true piety.

The texts quoted are already known (W 11, 13; CN 8, 11–12).
But Fénelon's conclusion, which followed immediately, demon-
strates his esteem for Lawrence:

> Here is, Your Excellency, the central proposition of my book
> that at first may seem the most difficult to the reader. But God
> permitted that it was one of those propositions supported by the
> greatest authorities of the saints of all ages.

34. In the same reply (second *Letter*), Fénelon spoke of the
"final throes of such a harsh torment" that St. Francis de Sales endured, of his "apparent belief" that heaven was closed to him, and
of "his terrible resolution, namely, to love God here below, assuming that he would no longer love him in the next life," a most "disinterested" act. At that moment his belief was invincible; before the
moment of grace no spiritual director could have taken his suffering away from him. Fénelon addressed Bossuet directly before referring to Lawrence (III, p. 392):

> What would you have said to the saint? The formal dogma
> of faith? He would not have doubted it at all. You would have
> *crucified him again,* to speak like Blessed John of the Cross.

This was *not the remedy for his suffering.* He found no *support in any doctrine or spiritual master.* In the end, *in the final throes of such a harsh torment, he had to make a terrible resolution,* the only one that would deliver the saint from his suffering.

We see how Brother Lawrence likewise overcame the trial: "In the intense sufferings that he had for four years, so intense that no one in the world could have convinced him he was saved..., he consoled himself by saying: Come what may, I will at least do everything for the rest of my life for the love of God; and thus forgetting himself, he resolved to lose himself for God, and this worked to his advantage" (W 13).

If you had been the director of this solitary saint, you would have *crucified him again.* You would have reasoned with him in vain; your reasonings would not have accomplished *what no one in the world could ever have done,* I mean, to *relieve him of the sense that he was damned.* What consoled him and delivered him from his *apparent* belief? It was his *forgetting* himself and his *being resolved to lose himself for God.*

...It probably took Saint Francis de Sales some time before he was able to make this *terrible resolution.* He only did it in the most extreme necessity. It was only *in the final throes of so harsh a torment, that in the end* he had to make what you call a *kind of sacrifice* or an *act of such disinterested love.* Would he not have been troubled and scandalized if he were required to make this terrible resolution before these *ultimate sufferings* occurred? Would you want to advise all kinds of good souls facing the perils of damnation to say like Brother Lawrence: *Come what may?* Would they not be scandalized? Must they not wait until *God moves them by particular touches and demands these kinds of sacrifices by his impetus,* to *help* these souls *bring them forth?* By anticipating the time, are we not thrusting them into anxiety and scandal?

35. Fénelon was advised to "go from the defensive to the offensive." He went over the different possibilities in his mind. Should he denounce, in addition to certain statements taken from Bossuet's works, some statements taken from the writings of de Noailles as well? Should he even take some statements from the *Life* of Brother Lawrence, approved by de Noailles, "without naming the authors?"

These were the questions he asked himself in his letter of January 16, 1699 to Father de Chanterac in Rome (IX, pp. 392–393):

> After what I said so deliberately in the *Réponse* [Reply] to the *Quæstiuncula,* I cannot and must not make myself the accuser of the Bishop of Meaux [Bossuet] concerning his works; but if the incident lasts long enough to allow the time for it, you can let loose some religious who was defender of doctrine and who might submit it to the Holy Office. He would have to present a certain number of statements taken from this prelate's books, and the thing must be done in the most proper manner, to eliminate all suspicion that I was the instigator of this process. It is not at all to my liking, but an old man of singular wisdom and piety, whom you have known in Paris for forty years, got this advice to me in a roundabout way as a means of promptly cutting the Gordian knot. He referred here to the story of the Congregations "de auxiliis" [on actual grace]. The Dominicans had a very powerful party in Rome; the agreement was already made by the majority of the examiners to decide against the Jesuits; Molina's book seemed without support, and therefore the Jesuits went from the defensive to the offensive. Immediately, that changed the appearance of the incident; they ended up by leaving everything in suspense and by imposing silence on the two parties. This is the story they related, and based on which they claim that we would have the same success.
>
> In the event they can find a zealous accuser, we will have to collect everything I called attention to in all my *Letters* against the bishop of Meaux. We will also have to weigh carefully whether it would be appropriate to take extracts from the *Life* of Brother Lawrence and from the *Pastoral Letter* of the archbishop of Paris [de Noailles]. We could also see the place where de Noailles said that the saints in heaven may only know God by what he is not. Do we know in the divine essence, by intuitive vision, only what it is not? To see God face to face, and not in obscurity, to know as we are known, is this to know in God only what he is not? Once again we must carefully weigh whether it would be appropriate to submit as well to the archbishop of Paris. That would be more irritating but it would resolve this more effectively. My first thought would be to submit a collection of all these statements without naming the authors. Consult some wise people about this who are well-acquainted with the Court where you are.

They wrote from Paris that Madame Guyon died at the Bastille.[1] I must say, now that she is dead, just as while she was alive, that everything I knew of her edified me.

NOTE

1. At the prison of the Bastille where she was detained. The news was false. Madame Guyon would die on June 9, 1717. Fénelon died on January 7, 1715.

36. An anonymous theologian[1] close to Bishop Godet des Marais published a letter against Fénelon, and the reaction came in two *Lettres de Monseigneur l'Archevêque duc de Cambrai à Monseigneur l'Évêque de Chartres, en réponse à celle d'un théologien* [Letters from His Excellency the Archbishop Duke of Cambrai to His Excellency the Bishop of Chartres, in response to that of a theologian] (III, pp. 162–189). Lawrence was mentioned there (III, p. 171): "Brother Lawrence certainly mortified himself every day. But the mortifications were *absolutely useless* during the four years when *he believed he was surely damned, when no one in the world could have convinced him otherwise,* and when he could only calm the temptation by saying: *Come what may,* etc." What an example of detached love (III, p. 188):

> What will you say when this fine friar assures you "that ecstasy and rapture belong only to the soul that takes delight in the gift, instead of rejecting it and going to God beyond his gift" (CN 10)? You will perhaps reply, Your Excellency, that so many saints have spoken only of renouncing the gifts, without ceasing to desire, by a sentiment of grace, the gifts necessary to unite themselves with God. This is explicitly stated in what I have said and for which I am being reproached. This much-criticized statement deals only with an apparent loss of gifts, and of a real sacrifice of oneself entirely, where God is found more purely than ever.

NOTE

1. Who is the "anonymous" theologian? A letter from Bossuet to his nephew on January 19, 1699, reveals his identity (Bossuet, *Oeuvres*, VI, p. 616): "The

bishop of Chartres and I are decidedly of the same opinion, since he approved my book *États d'oraison* [States of Prayer] in which I said everything; and among other things, that you could in no reasonable act eradicate the motive of beatitude, for the ultimate end, implicitly or explicitly. When it is not explicit, it is then that the motives are separated *per mentem*, as you say, but never truly nor otherwise by abstraction; which is ultimately what I said. But the bishop of Chartres did not go as far as I did in the explanation and in the development of these fine principles. You will soon see a reply from him under the name of a theologian who raised the question, but, since he did not have the leisure to do the work himself, I did it."

37. At Rome, opinions remained divided. Innocent XII wanted to stall for time; he hesitated to pronounce against the Archbishop of Cambrai's book, to which he was sympathetic. There was talk of a project of "canons," rules for the spiritual life. The pressure coming from France, however, was indeed great. Bossuet wrote to his nephew on March 16, 1699 (Bossuet, *Oeuvres*, VI, p. 658): "You will see by the prompt departure of this mail, specially dispatched, how the King has taken the news of the project of the canons. I am sending you the *Mémoire* that we have composed where you will find the reasons that have moved this Prince. He received it this morning. We spoke to him, the Archbishop [de Noailles] of Paris and myself, along the same lines, but at different times." The same day, Archbishop de Noailles wrote to Father Bossuet (the nephew) at Rome (VI, p. 660): "this morning I informed the King of everything you told me. His Majesty easily understood the disadvantages of this fine project.... The King would not have what he asked for and what was promised him so many times, and he would have the pain of seeing the evil he wanted to cure increase. He sought, for more than two years, to have a clear, precise decision, and he would only have general rules, always easy to elude, that would not so much attack the book in question, but rather, the most ancient works of false mysticism. I find, furthermore, that this decision does not foster the glory of the Pope or the honor of the Holy See, for it cannot be honorable, that after so long and solemn an investigation of a book that can be read in three hours, it would appear to the whole Church that no one dares judge it...." But the *Mémoire* prepared by Bossuet (the text can be found in VI, p. 661), where the King asked

to "put an end, once and for all, ...to the disputes that inflame his kingdom," would have no effect. The decision was already made, though no one in Paris knew.

From Rome, Father Bossuet wrote on March 13, 1699 (VI, p. 653): "God is stronger than men, and thus the truth has triumphed." A brief dated March 12, 1699 (and not a more solemn "bull" as desired by Fénelon's adversaries) condemned the book, from which twenty-three statements were taken, though none, however, were declared "heretical." Once he became aware of the text of the brief, Fénelon submitted on April 9, 1699.

Brother Lawrence will be referred to yet one more time in a text by Fénelon in 1712 for Pope Clement XI, where he explained himself regarding Pure Love and the conflict with Bossuet: *Dissertatio de Amore puro seu Analysis controversiae inter Archiepiscopum cameracensem et meldensem Episcopum habitae de charitatis natura, necnon de habituali statu puri amoris* (III, pp. 420–571). Fénelon quoted two passages from Brother Lawrence (CN 13 and 26 in III, p. 525; and W 10 and 11 in III, p. 527) not without indicating that he was "mirifice laudatus," highly praised by Cardinal de Noailles.

38. It would be appropriate to conclude with Fénelon's testimony on Brother Lawrence, taken from his letter of August 5, 1700 (VIII, p. 623), where the Archbishop of Cambrai recounted to the Countess of Montberon his meeting with Lawrence in 1690 or 1691. Fénelon had loaned Lawrence's *Life* to the Countess.

> You have seen many saints that love instructed without learning, for no trace of a human hand was to be found there. It is not astonishing that love teaches us to love. Those who love sincerely, and whom the Spirit of God inebriates with his new wine, speak an entirely new language. When you feel what others do not feel, and what you yourself have not felt before, you express this the best way you can, and almost always find that the expression only partly conveys the reality. Should the church find that you express yourself incorrectly, you are ready to correct yourself, and you have only docility, only simplicity as your testament. You do not cling to terms or ideas. A soul that loves in

the true spirit of renunciation does not want to retain its language or its insights. You can take nothing from someone who wants to have nothing of his own.

...I am in no hurry to have the books back; read them only when you have nothing better to do. Perhaps you won't mind rereading them at certain times, or at least to review some parts of them. These inspirations of grace, so original in themselves, are not exactly what you experience; it is, nonetheless, something from the same source. The words of the saints themselves are indeed different from the discourse of those who tried to describe them. Saint Catherine of Genoa was prodigious in love. Brother Lawrence was rough by nature yet sensitive by grace. This mixture was admirable and revealed God present in him. I saw him, and there is a place in the book where the author, without naming me, related in a few words an excellent conversation I had with him on death, when he was very sick yet quite content.

Regarding Brother Lawrence's posthumous impact, Fénelon's veneration for him greatly contributed to making him known abroad, as we have explained in the General Introduction to this work.

Select Bibliography
of Related Works in English

I. Some Editions of Brother Lawrence in English (by year)

The Practice of the Presence of God, Being the Conversations, Letters, and Spiritual Maxims of Brother Lawrence of the Resurrection. Newly translated by Donald Attwater. London: Burns, Oates and Washbourne, 1926, 1948, 1977, etc.; Springfield, IL: Templegate, 1959, 1962. (Later editions include preface by Dorothy Day.)

The Practice of the Presence of God. Translated by Sr. Mary David, SSND. Westminster, MD: Newman Press, 1945; Ramsey, NJ: Paulist Press, 1978.

The Practice of the Presence of God and Selections from the Little Flowers of St. Francis. Edited by Hugh Martin. London: SCM Press, 1956.

The Practice of the Presence of God, Being Conversations and Letters of Brother Lawrence. Old Tappan, NJ: Fleming H. Revell Co., Spire Books, 1958. (Apparently based on 1897 translation.)

The Practice of the Presence of God. Illustrated by Jeff Hill. Vernon, NY: Peter Pauper Press, 1967.

The God Illuminated Cook: A New Edition of The Practice of the Presence of God *by Brother Lawrence.* Edited by Robin Dawes, et al. Hankin, NY: Strength Books, East Ridge Press, 1975.

The Practice of the Presence of God. Edited by Donald E. Demaray and Brother Lawrence. Devotional Classics Series. Grand Rapids, MI: Baker Book House, 1975.

The Practice of the Presence of God. Translated with an Introduction by John J. Delaney. With a Foreword by Henri J. M. Nouwen. New York: Image Books, Doubleday, 1977.

The Practice of the Presence of God. Translated by Robert J. Edmonson. Edited by Hal M. Helms. Rev. ed. Orleans, MA: Paraclete Press, 1985.

The Practice of the Presence of God: The Conversations, Letters, Ways, and Spiritual Principles of Brother Lawrence, from his Own Literary Remains and the Writings of Joseph de Beaufort. Translated by E. M. Blaiklock. London: Hodder & Stoughton, 1986.

II. Excerpts and Commentaries

Cheney, Sheldon. *Men Who Have Walked With God, Being the Story of Mysticism Through the Ages Told in the Biographies of Representative Seers and Saints with Excerpts from their Writings and Sayings.* New York: Alfred A. Knopf, 1956.

Douglas, Elmer, trans. *The Kitchen Saint and the Heritage of Islam: Incorporating the* Practice of the Presence of God, *by Brother Lawrence, with Notes by the Translator.* Princeton Theological Monograph Series, no. 18. Allison Park, PA: Pickwick Publications, 1989.

Edwards, Gene, ed. *Practicing His Presence: Brother Lawrence and Frank Laubach.* Augusta, ME: Christian Books, 1973.

Freer, Harold Wiley. *God Meets Us Where We Are: An Interpretation of Brother Lawrence.* Nashville, TN: Abingdon Press, 1967.

Giallanza, Joel. "The Wisdom of Brother Lawrence." *Mount Carmel* 32 (1984): 158-164.

Lantry, Jerome. "Brother Lawrence and the Presence of God." *Carmelite Digest* 1 (1986): 44-51.

Llewelyn, Robert A., ed. *Daily Readings with Brother Lawrence.* Springfield, IL: Templegate Publishers, 1986.

Maas, Robin. "Practicing the Presence of God: Recollection in the Carmelite Tradition." *Spiritual Life* 36 (1990): 99-107.

Maccise, Camilo. "Lawrence of the Resurrection." *Carmelite Digest* 7 (1992): 55-63.

May, Gerald G. *The Awakened Heart: Opening Yourself to the Love You Need.* San Francisco: Harper San Francisco, 1991.

Parkhurst, Louis Gifford, ed. *The Believer's Secret of the Abiding Presence: Compiled from the Writings of Andrew Murray and Brother Lawrence.* Minneapolis, MN: Bethany House Publications, 1987.

Williams, Michael, ed. *The Walked With God: A Newly Revised and Abridged Edition of "The Book of Christian Classics."* Greenwich, CT: Fawcett, 1962.

Winter, David. *Closer Than a Brother: Brother Lawrence for Today.* Wheaton, IL: Harold Shaw Publishers, 1981.

The Institute of Carmelite Studies promotes research and publication in the field of Carmelite spirituality. Its members are Discalced Carmelites, part of a Roman Catholic community—frars, nuns, and laity—who are heirs to the teaching and way of life of Teresa of Jesus and John of the Cross, men and women dedicated to contemplation and to ministry in the church and the world. Information concerning their way of life is available through local diocesan Vocation Offices, or from the Vocation Director's Office, 1525 Carmel Road, Hubertus, WI, 53033.